Making an Impact Outside of the Classroom

T0243360

Educators, you can continue to make an impact after you're ready to leave the classroom! This handy, comprehensive resource will help you explore alternative career paths in education that will still allow you to use the skillsets and unique qualifications you developed as a teacher or leader.

Bestselling author Starr Sackstein begins by helping you decide whether you want to move into another position or leave altogether. She then shows you how to seek opportunities, take risks, network, and prepare for interviews. Next, she presents a wide variety of career pathways for educators, including school and district-based options, consulting work, EdTech opportunities, publishing jobs, higher education, and more!

Starr also answers frequently asked questions such as how much you should charge and whether you need additional degrees. Throughout, there are fascinating case studies highlighting people who have left to do alternate jobs and their top takeaways. An accompanying video series offers even more advice from a wide variety of educators who have switched roles. With this helpful guide, you'll feel empowered to courageously restart – and continue to leave a legacy in education.

Starr Sackstein is a recovering perfectionist who is an assessment reforming enthusiast. Currently, she is the COO of Mastery Portfolio, an EdTech startup committed to helping schools move to standard-based communication. She was a high school English and journalism teacher for 16 years, a lead humanities learner for two years, a publisher and developmental editor, and social media manager. Starr is an author, blogger, and speaker committed to changing the way we do assessment nationally and globally. You can learn more about her work on her website MsSackstein.com, and you can follow her on X, formerly known as Twitter @MsSackstein.

Making an Impact Outside of the Classroom

A Complete Guide to the Exciting Job Possibilities for Educators

Starr Sackstein

Routledge
Taylor & Francis Group

NEW YORK AND LONDON

Designed cover image: © Getty Images

First published 2025
by Routledge
605 Third Avenue, New York, NY 10158

and by Routledge
4 Park Square, Milton Park, Abingdon, Oxon, OX14 4RN

Routledge is an imprint of the Taylor & Francis Group, an informa business

ISBN: 978-1-032-58556-7 (pbk)
ISBN: 978-1-003-45070-2 (ebk)

DOI: 10.4324/9781003450702

Typeset in CelesteST
by SPi Technologies India Pvt Ltd (Straive)

Access the Support Material: www.routledge.com/9781032585567

For anyone who has thought about leaving the classroom but wasn't sure where to go next, this book was written for you.

For everyone who loves the art of teaching but is struggling in the current climate, this book is for you.

For every educator, you are more qualified than you know, and you are appreciated more than it seems. Your impact changes the world.

Thank you.

Contents

Support Material

The tools in the appendix of this book are also available for download from our website, so you can easily print them for your own use. To access them, go to the book's product page at routledge.com/9781032585567 and click on the link that says Support Material.

Bonus: The book is also accompanied by video interviews of educators describing their new job opportunities. More are being added on a regular basis. To access this exciting video library, go to https://www.youtube.com/playlist?list=PLYKvoWou3e6L326jJgqTucJ39znIV6rz8

About the Author

 **Starr Sackstein** started her teaching career at Far Rockaway High School in the early 2000s, eager to make a difference. Quickly learning to connect with students, she recognized the most important part of teaching: building relationships. Fostering relationships with students and peers to encourage community growth and a deeper understanding of personal contribution through reflection, she has continued to elevate her students by putting them at the center of the learning.

Sackstein worked as the Director of Humanities (Business, English, Library, Reading, Social Studies, and World Languages) in West Hempstead, New York. While in her first year of leadership, she completed her advanced leadership certification at SUNY New Paltz. Taking what she learned in classes and applying her classroom leadership to a team of teachers, Sackstein started growing as a new school leader, building relationships and demonstrating the kind of leadership she would have liked from her past administrators. From this experience, she wrote *From Teacher to Leader: Finding Your Way as a First-Time Leader without Losing Your Mind.*

Before her leadership role, Sackstein was a UFT Teacher Center coordinator and ELA teacher at Long Island City High

School in New York. She also spent nine years at World Journalism Preparatory School in Flushing, New York, as a high school English and journalism teacher, where her students ran the multimedia news outlet WJPSnews.com. In 2011, the Dow Jones News Fund honored Starr as a Special Recognition Adviser, and in 2012, *Education Update* recognized her as an outstanding educator. Sackstein has thrown out grades; teaching students learning isn't about numbers but about developing skills and articulating growth.

In 2012, Sackstein tackled National Board Certification to reflect on her practice and grow as an educational English facilitator. After a year of closely examining her work with students, she was honored. She is also a certified Master Journalism Educator through the Journalism Education Association (JEA). Sackstein also served as the New York State Director to JEA from 2010–2016, helping advisers in New York enhance journalism programs.

She is the author of *Teaching Mythology Exposed: Helping Teachers Create Visionary Classroom Perspective*; *Blogging for Educators*; *Teaching Students to Self-Assess: How Do I Help Students Grow as Learners?*; *The Power of Questioning: Opening Up the World of Student Inquiry*; *Hacking Assessment: 10 Ways to Go Gradeless in a Traditional Grades School*; and *Hacking Homework: 10 Strategies That Inspire Learning Outside of the Classroom* co-written with Connie Hamilton. Starr has published *Peer Feedback in the Classroom: Empower Students to be the Experts* with the Association for Supervision and Curriculum Development (ASCD). Sackstein published *From Teacher to Leader: Finding Your Way as a First-Time Leader without Losing Your Mind* in 2019 (DBC). In 2021, Sackstein co-authored *Hacking Learning Centers in Grades 6–12: How to Design Small-Group Instruction to Foster Active Learning, Shared Leadership, and Student Accountability* with Karen Terwilliger, as well as authoring *Assessing with Respect: Everyday Practices that Meet Students' Social and Emotional Needs* (ASCD). Sackstein contributed to compilation works in 2017 and 2018: *Education Write Now*, edited by Jeff Zoul and Joe Mazza, and *10 Perspectives on Innovation in Education* with Routledge. Her most recent contribution to an edited volume is in *Ungrading: Why Rating Students Undermines Learning (and What to Do Instead) (Teaching and Learning in Higher Education)* (West Virginia University Press, 2020).

She blogged for *Education Week Teacher* at "Work in Progress," where she discussed all aspects of being a teacher and education reform for five years ending in 2019. She made the Bammy Awards finals for Secondary High School Educator in 2014 and for blogging in 2015. At speaking engagements worldwide, Starr speaks about blogging, journalism education, bringing your own device, and throwing out grades, which was also highlighted in a recent TEDx talk entitled "A Recovering Perfectionist's Journey to Give up Grades." In 2016, she was named one of ASCD's Emerging Leaders.

In recent years, Sackstein has spoken internationally in Canada, Dubai, France, South Korea, and Spain on various topics, from assessment reform to technology-enhanced language instruction. Several of her books have also been translated into Japanese.

Sackstein began consulting full time with the Core Collaborative in 2019, working with teams on assessment reform and bringing student voice to the front of all classroom learning. It is through her affiliation with the Core Collaborative that Sackstein became the publisher with Mimi and Todd Press, helping other authors share their voices around making an impact for students. The first publication she worked on was *Belonging Through a Culture of Dignity: The Keys to Successful Equity Implementation* by Dr. Floyd Cobb and John J. Krownapple. Most recently, *Arrows: A Systems-Based Approach to School Leadership* by Carrie Rosebrock and Sarah Henry was released through Mimi and Todd Press.

Mastery Portfolio, an EdTech startup, named Sackstein their COO in August 2021. Mastery Portfolio is an EdTech startup that helps teachers and schools change the way they report learning in alignment with Sackstein's core beliefs about grades and standards-based assessment. Through this new role, Starr is hoping to really impact the learning experiences of students all over the world.

Balancing a busy career of writing and educating with being the mom of Logan is a challenging adventure. Seeing the world through his eyes reminds her why education needs to change for every child.

Rounding out her family is her husband Charlie who is a mindfulness and meditation coach as well as a personal trainer, which comes in handy for being conscious of self-care. Together they adventure around the world bringing harmony to each other's lives.

Starr can be reached at mssackstein@gmail.com or via X at @MsSackstein. She can also be found at MsSackstein.com.

Foreword

What do I want to be when I grow up? My oldest memory of that reply is "princess." My parents were business owners, so for many years I thought I would step in as the owner of a local office supply store as my career. My 18-year-old self was on a path to earn an aerospace engineering degree from Michigan State University. I actually considered waiting tables forever, but I wanted a lifestyle I knew the restaurant business couldn't offer. I saw the headaches the owners of Signatures American Grill suffered and I thought, NO WAY do I want to open my own restaurant. So I filled my schedule at MSU with general education requirements and changed my major three times before landing on education and earning my bachelor's degree.

The titles I held in my career are plenty. Elementary teacher, middle school teacher, instructional coach, secondary assistant principal, middle school principal, elementary principal, district curriculum director. Now, my signature includes author, speaker, coach/consultant. As a young teacher, I never thought I'd leave the classroom. *Making an Impact Outside of the Classroom* will walk you through a cognitive journey to explore and reflect on where your professional path will lead. I had no doubt I would be successful; I was built with a strong drive to succeed. However, it's almost comical how many times I was wrong about what I thought my next role would be.

I suppose looking at my resume, people might assume it was my intention to keep moving up, climbing the metaphorical ladder. The truth is that I was so vested in the role I had in the moment, and being the best I could be at it, that I didn't take time to consider what might be next. Instead, I was constantly reflecting and looking for ways to improve the role I had. In hindsight, I was, like most educators, pretty tough on myself, focusing on what I *couldn't* do well, rather than on the achievements I'd made. It turns out that those quiet accomplishments prepared me better than I thought for a career I never imagined.

Making Moves

The decision to leave the classroom isn't an easy one. I can recall both the push and pull factors that brought changes to my career. Sometimes I felt called or inspired to embrace a new role. Other times I found myself unhappy in the work I was doing. My committee work on school improvement and curriculum teams gave me glimpses of education beyond my classroom. One opportunity I had was to work with the State Department on grade-level content expectations. One of the leaders of the team compared curriculum work to a sausage, saying "some people just can't watch it be made." That comment made me aware of a unique interest I had that perhaps all educators didn't love, so I paid more attention to opportunities for me to apply that passion in various ways.

Contributions I made to the overall school success kindled a curiosity in administration. I followed that interest and took my first position as an assistant principal in a middle school where my primary role was student discipline – not instructional leadership. I found it challenging to make long-term impacts around student achievement when I was buried under what seemed like mountains of referrals every day. I knew this was not the best fit for me long term. However, I had little experience in administration; I had a toddler and a preschooler at home and was pregnant with my third child – not the time for a career change. So, I didn't act on the urges to leave the AP position, but there was no denying they were there.

In many instances, it was my choice to leave or take on the positions I ultimately held. However, happenstance landed me behind the principal's desk only 18 months after starting my job as AP. During that time of my life I wasn't oozing confidence, so my leadership style was more about proving myself to my peers, many of whom had been teaching longer than me. As you can imagine, it made my role more challenging. These first two administrative positions would classify as the biggest failures of my career. The half-full side of that is there is truth in learning quickly and deeply from your mistakes (more on that in the next section).

The pushes and pulls from different roles continued until someone asked me what position I would have when I retired. I hadn't mindfully taken a Stephen Covey approach to begin with the end in mind when it came to my career. Just the process of considering what I loved, where my strengths were, and how I wanted to contribute to the education profession shifted my push and pull cycle to pull-pull-pull. Today, I feel fortunate that all my options and choices are opportunities that pull me in new directions rather than push me away from unsatisfying jobs.

The draw to curriculum and instruction led me to presenting at small local conferences. That rekindled my desire to teach, so leading professional learning expanded beyond my own school. Eventually, I had so much content to share that I was pulled to publish. Never did I imagine I would be a bestselling author. During my journey, I saw myself becoming a princess, a business owner, an electrical engineer, an accountant, and a superintendent – none of which I ever achieved, and I couldn't be more grateful that I didn't.

Transferable Skills

Over the years, I've gained a significant amount of knowledge and understanding around curriculum, instruction, and other aspects of education. That expertise is easy to recognize and measure. I can identify some of the "aha" moments that changed my teaching or leadership style. Yet, looking back now, there are softer skills that have developed from my failures and successes. Attributes such as patience, communication skills, large and small picture thinking, and collaboration strengthened and have served me well in my role today.

The ability to establish structures and routines extends far beyond the classroom expectations. It allowed me to look at when a system is needed and when to provide autonomy. The most common comment I receive working with teachers and school leaders today is that they feel more intentional about decisions they make every day. That focus on purpose and strategy was fostered throughout my experiences in the classroom and administration.

Reinforced through my failures and successes is the notion of being relevant. People must know how and/or why decisions are made, initiatives are launched, and plans are developed or assessed. Without relevance, it's challenging to build a team who understands the value of their mission. It's another understated eye I developed by teaching with clarity and leading with transparency.

Talking, collaborating, challenging, supporting, and inspiring other educators is the conversational voice I bring to my books. The title "author" is one that I'm proud of, likely because it wasn't even on my radar as a possibility that I would have something to share that other people would be interested in hearing. However, the face-to-face interactions provided a counter-narrative to my self-doubt.

My professional path began as a teacher, then led to administrative roles, and now I am an author and consultant. However, the abilities we develop as educators are transferable to countless other careers and Starr Sackstein offers many suggestions for you to consider. Don't dismiss the notion that you could have as much success in business or an education-related industry. After negotiating contracts for my school district, I considered being an educational attorney. The point is that teaching and education opens more doors than you might think. If you are being pushed or pulled in another direction, as I suspect you are or you wouldn't be reading this book, the place where you leave the biggest mark might be yet to come.

What's Next?

For now, I plan to enjoy where I am professionally. I wake up every day loving my place in education with a feeling that I'm making a contribution to the best profession on the planet. In my 50+ years of life, I've learned that opportunities present themselves in unexpected places and at unexpected times. The approach in my later years has been to strive to be the best I can be while diligently looking to grow in a variety of areas. When a connection, opportunity, or event piques my interest, I do what all good questioners do ... I get curious and engage in exploration through the lens of inquiry. My greatest joy is when another educator connects their success with an "aha" moment that was inspired by my work.

Thanks to Starr Sackstein, you can use this book to help you find new doors to share the talents teaching has provided you. Or, perhaps, you will decide to remain in the classroom for now or forever. Whatever you decide, whenever you decide it, know that there isn't a set path for your professional future. George Washington Carver is quoted as saying, "Education is the key to unlock the golden door of freedom." As a professional educator, you not only open doors for your students, but you also hold the key to your own future. This book will help you see what's on the other side of your door.

Connie Hamilton
Author, Speaker, Coach/Consultant

Acknowledgments

No book is written alone regardless of whose name is on the cover. A big thank you to Lauren Davis who I've been eager to work with for a long time now. I hope to have more opportunities to work with you.

Thank you to the many educators who answered my call when I asked for your time. Almost 100 educators answered my survey. Your experiences helped to make this book what it is.

I'd like to thank the educators who took the survey one step farther and took the time to hop on a call with me to be interviewed to be a part of the playlist for the folks who are reading this book. Your stories and experiences will no doubt help educators who are trying to make good decisions about what direction to go next. So I'd like to shout out Walter McKenzie, my long-time friend, colleague, and mentor who has been my champion for many years. When I turn on the bat signal, Walter always answers. Lindsay Prendergast, my ISTE community partner in crime and fellow edchamp. MaryAnn DeRosa, who has become a great friend and continues to inspire me on so many levels. Chris McNutt, who is doing important work in humanizing education. Diana Laufenberg whose innovative approaches to education continue to inspire. Kayla Solinsky who makes me smile and supports all kinds of educators in a variety of different ways. Constance Borro, my business partner and committee educator who helped me transition into business. Jonathan Frye, who does inspired instructional design. Harris Lee whose inspiring story of personal loss grew into advocacy. Thank you to the additional folks who recorded interviews with me after this book has already gone to print. Although you aren't mentioned by name, I appreciate you and I know the folks reading this do too.

A second round of thank yous go to Katie Harrison for always being a reader of my work early and providing feedback. Connie Hamilton who has been my rock through so many changes in the past. Alexandra Laing whose tenacity and commitment continue to inspire me.

A special thanks to Gretchen Oltman and the EdChamps, this group of educators is my tribe, and I'm so lucky to have all of you in my life both professionally and personally.

And a hearty bit of gratitude goes to my husband Charlie Anstadt and my son Logan Miller who are the most supportive, loving human beings. No matter what kind of crazy turns my career takes, they are my greatest cheerleaders.

Thank you, thank you. Thank you!

Introduction

Preparing for the Future in an Evolving World

We often speak of preparing students for careers that may or may not exist already in today's classrooms. Being called upon to innovate and make predictions of what the future holds, each educator is uniquely challenged to imagine and engage in speculative activities that improve our young people's likelihood of success in the future. Unfortunately, when we taught our current teachers, few took the time to undergo the same activity. Education has functioned the same way for the longest time, and so has our preparation for that career. The biggest decisions we had to make were around what age group we wanted to work with and where and figuring out the content area that speaks to our passions.

In the post-COVID-19 world we live in, the culture of many educational institutions has changed, and there has been an increase in folks struggling to remain excited about their classroom or district-based work. This struggle doesn't define the love you feel for your students or colleagues or maybe even teaching. Still, it has been increasingly harder to ignore challenges that make the day-to-day depression or anxiety-inducing. When I was in the classroom, I loved teaching – heck, I still love the idea of being in the classroom. When photos from the past come up in my timeline or former students and colleagues reach out, there will always be a part of me that longs for that version of my career, that version of my identity. However, leaving my last district-based position set me on a path that I couldn't have imagined, and that I am still exploring as more time ticks on.

DOI: 10.4324/9781003450702-1

1

My path reminds me of the Beatles' song *The Long and Winding Road* as my heart has always been in education, and many of my career choices have led me back to elements of it even though I no longer have a classroom I can call my own.

Ironically, just because I find myself where I am right now doesn't mean that I won't wind up back in a school or district in the future. One thing I have learned about this journey is that there is no one right path and that the path itself is ever-changing, as am I and probably you too. To that end, I doubt anyone gets into education thinking they will leave it prior to retirement, but many of us do end up leaving the classroom.

Educators exiting the profession is a complex issue influenced by a combination of factors that can vary from one individual to another. Some of the main reasons educators at all levels are leaving the profession include:

- **Low Pay**: Teaching is often less financially rewarding than other professions requiring similar levels of education and training. Many teachers struggle to make ends meet, especially considering the time and effort they invest in their work and the money we pour into our classrooms for supplies and materials that our schools can't provide. Additionally, many of us work multiple jobs to ensure we can provide good lives for our families and ourselves. This is an area, I recently learned, that has advocacy groups working to improve. If this is something you're passionate about, why not get involved too?
- **High Workload and Stress**: Educators at every level face heavy workloads that include lesson planning, grading, administrative tasks, and extracurricular responsibilities. The pressure to meet curriculum standards and achieve positive student outcomes can lead to burnout and high stress levels. For administrators, there are additional external stresses from the community that increase visibility and commentary on decisions that are made well or not. Navigating the political climate and trying to please everyone can sometimes take the focus off what matters the most – the students.

- **Lack of Respect and Recognition**: Teachers often feel undervalued and underappreciated by society, policy-makers, and even parents. The lack of respect and recognition for their critical role in shaping the future can be demoralizing. Many of us thought this might change after COVID-19 given how hard it was for families to educate their kids; unfortunately, expectations have continued to increase, and the grace one would hope for within it hasn't improved.
- **Lack of Autonomy and Creativity**: Increasing emphasis on standardized testing and rigid curricula can limit teachers' ability to design creative and engaging lessons that cater to their students' individual needs and interests. It can be quite stifling to be handed a pacing guide with a curriculum already written with the expectation to be in lockstep with colleagues. We all understand the need for equity across classrooms, but each teacher should be given the kind of professional courtesy owed to make a space unique and personalized for the kids they teach.
- **Limited Career Advancement**: In some educational systems, career advancement opportunities for teachers can be limited, leading to frustration and a lack of motivation to stay in the profession. It takes a genuinely innovative teacher to find alternative pathways to develop as an educator. Personally, when I didn't get what I needed in my school building, rather than leave, I joined national education organizations and started to get involved there. For example, I joined ASCD, ISTE, JEA, NCTE, and more to be around like-minded folks I could grow from. I also did National Board Certification to challenge myself in a unique way. This one choice positively changed my career in ways I could probably write a whole other book about.
- **Inadequate Professional Development**: Teachers require ongoing training and development to stay up to date with best practices and new teaching methods. A lack of meaningful professional development opportunities can hinder their growth and effectiveness. As mentioned above, if any educator wants to be more than *just* a regular classroom teacher, many times they have to find the learning

spaces themselves; they may even need to pay for it themselves if the school doesn't have the funds to send them.

- **Classroom Management Challenges**: Dealing with behavioral issues and maintaining a positive classroom environment can be exhausting. In some cases, the lack of support in managing disruptive students can contribute to teacher burnout. This has been exceptionally true as of late. COVID-19 has changed the way students participate in learning, creating an atmosphere that is less about learning and more about managing, which can take some of the joy of teaching away.

- **Lack of Resources**: Teachers often face shortages of essential resources, from classroom supplies to up-to-date technology. This can hinder their ability to provide quality education and create engaging learning environments. Notably, this is true as it pertains to school infrastructures around technology. There are few things more frustrating than unreliable technology, especially when you are trying to do something new.

- **Parent and Community Pressure**: Teachers sometimes face unrealistic expectations from parents and community members, which can create additional stress and tension. Leaders suffer this fate as well. Unfortunately, folks who aren't in education really don't understand the realities of what we do. This is why authentic educator voices need to be shared.

- **Changing Education Policies**: Frequent changes in education policies, standards, and curriculum requirements can create uncertainty and frustration for teachers, as they need to constantly adapt their teaching methods and content to meet new expectations. The biggest frustration with issues like this is often how changes are made but aren't communicated consistently. Couple that with the reality that there is inadequate training on new expectations, many educators don't even realize they are doing something "wrong" until a formal evaluation informs them.

- **Work–Life Balance**: The demands of teaching, including after-hours grading and lesson planning, can infringe on teachers' personal time and family life, leading to a poor work–life balance. I would take this one step further and say that it is tough to stop working after official school hours, and if you have a family at home, they often feel like you are prioritizing work. Most educators always feel like the workday continues.

- **Lack of Support**: Teachers need robust support systems from administrators, colleagues, and parents. A lack of support in handling classroom challenges or addressing their professional needs can contribute to feelings of isolation and dissatisfaction. Siloed teaching and learning environments are suitable for no one, yet most of us have experienced them in our careers. Most of us crave community, which is why social media has been so helpful when we don't get what we need from our work-school environments.

Addressing the issue of teachers leaving the profession requires a comprehensive approach that involves improving compensation, reducing workload, providing better professional development, enhancing respect and recognition, and creating a supportive and empowering environment for educators or else sustainability and longevity in education careers will no longer be a thing for the majority of folks who enter the field.

For the record, this book isn't being written to tell you to leave the classroom or education at large; this book is being written to help navigate our current landscape. I'm still hopeful that education will have another golden age where educators will be revered for our significant and challenging job. Although it is cliché to say, we are the heart of all careers – teachers are responsible for preparing most everyone for their chosen careers – and places like Finland understand that.

As you read this book, know that it isn't written as a narrative, so you don't have to go from chapter to chapter dutifully taking in every word. Rather, know where you are in your journey and, if you need to, skip around for what support you need right now. In each chapter, you can navigate through sub-head sections that are clearly labeled and reflection questions to help you make decisions about how to skip from place to place. Occasionally, there are suggested activities to help you make better-informed decisions as you move through your process.

Change can be scary, but it doesn't have to be – the more you know, the easier it becomes to take necessary risks. So now I invite you on this amazing adventure; I can't wait to hear where it takes you. In the immortal words of Dr. Seuss, "Oh, the places you'll go!"

1

To Leave or Not to Leave, That Is the Question

How Do You Know When to Leave?

When do you know it is time to leave the classroom – this place you love and have found a home in – a place you've fallen in and out of love with and a place known to break your heart and rebuild it in a day? How do you know when it is time to leave a place that largely defines who you are or, at some point, defined who you were?

The simple answer is: *you don't*.

There is no single right way to know when to or if you should leave. And regardless of the decision you make now, it doesn't have to be permanent. That is the beauty of life and the nature of change.

Like starting a family, no matter how much you prepare or *think* you prepare, the right time doesn't magically show up just because you think it should. The ebbs and flows of life don't usually provide those momentous sea-separating experiences to show you the way. Defining moments are usually less noticeable, and the key is knowing when to blindly jump into the abyss and brace for the coming impact.

Growing up, I never thought I'd be a teacher. But once I became one, I knew I could be nothing else. The career showed up like the glass slipper that was meant for my foot alone. I was defined, in part, by being a high school English teacher. A good class, a small shared exchange with a student, or a *thank you* could turn a bad day into a good one, and as I grew more confident in my craft, I could say I wished

DOI: 10.4324/9781003450702-2   7

I'd had a teacher like me when I was growing up. (And, over the years, I have amassed a drawer full of *thank yous* from parents *and* students to support my assertions.)

Despite my love of the classroom, I felt uneasy staying in the same position. I tend to bore easily, and I knew that if I wasn't growing, I was walking up the down escalator, not moving anywhere despite the effort – and that was *not* an option. I had considered changing positions, but I only vaguely thought about leaving the classroom; in fact, I specifically chose not to get my administrative license because I didn't want to have the option for a long time. Instead, I opted for National Board Certification to further my education and pushed myself harder by digging deeper into my craft. It wasn't until many years later that I would find a way to navigate into leadership in a way that made sense to me, even if it wasn't the typical path.

Foundational Shifts

During the 16 years I taught high school English, my belief system, practice, and philosophy evolved, propelling me in different directions at times despite my deep commitment to student learning. These tides of change in experiences colored how and what I thought in the classroom, and my perception adjusted accordingly, though I realized later that these shifts had to happen gradually if they were to be authentic and lasting.

The longer I spent in the classroom, exposed to different ideas, the more I shifted and started taking more risks. It is with both pride and shame that I admit the teacher I was when I left the classroom was barely recognizable to the one who had entered it in her early twenties. In my early career, I was deeply entrenched in dogma from my own learning experiences and didn't do enough to help all learners. Unfortunately, I was too ignorant and naive to see how my practice limited my students' growth. However, I was willing to learn from anyone and eager to truly listen to students, so the way I taught and thought improved and expanded. My whole concept of what it means to be an educator has shifted astronomically over the more than 20 years I have been in education now.

Signposts

Teachers consider leaving the classroom and maybe even the profession for various reasons. For some teachers, the first time they consider moving into leadership is when an administrator or colleague asks them to think about a change. Others, as I did, exhibit some of the signs below and feel prompted to move. (Although I mentioned a bunch of reasons in the introduction, I didn't make it specific to the classroom – this section will drill more deeply into what that looks like, feels like, and sounds like.)

Sign	Meaning
Boredom	You still love the kids, but you are bored with the lessons you teach and the routine of daily responsibilities you once found exciting. While this could lead to more risk-taking and research if you feel it could improve your job experience, it could mean it is time to try a new challenge.
Restlessness	You start looking at other professions – not just other jobs. You start thinking about how much of your life you've given to your current job and what you have learned from it. You're reflective, but not necessarily in a productive way. You have energy needing to be redirected, possibly the impetus to try something new. You must be bold if you stay where you are; restlessness can lead to poor decision-making.

Sign	Meaning
Irritability	You are bothered – perhaps irrationally – by things previously not troubling. You're easily upset, and your level of satisfaction from your work is consistently poor. You still love the kids but feel their behaviors are a personal affront. You also think you can do other people's jobs better than they can. When your patience starts to wane, look deeper into why.
Complacency	You start to *phone it in*. Things come easily to you, and you feel no need or desire to push harder because of other things happening in your life. You acknowledge this isn't the best version of yourself when you notice; you may even be nostalgic for previous times when you were great at your job. In fact, you want to return to the best version of yourself. Are you feeling burned out, and that is why you aren't trying as hard? Only you can figure out if pushing through this difficult time is best or if a new challenge will reinvigorate your interest in this career.

Sign	Meaning
Exhaustion or burnout	Perhaps you are burned out. It could look like complacency, but you honestly don't have anything left in the tank to give. It is likely you may even have a hard time remembering when you liked being in the classroom. Your whole attitude and posture about teaching have changed, and you are feeling nostalgic for another time. Or if you are already at full burnout, you may be taking a lot of time off even though you know that isn't good for your students or the community. There is no shame in admitting this may be where you are; you just may need a real break for some perspective.
Willingness to take risks	You take more calculated risks. You try new things and get more involved in professional learning outside of work. You readily apply what you learn because you want to be great at your job and don't have the fears new educators have. You have experience and a toolbox, and you're hungry for more.

Sign	Meaning
Constant questioning of purpose in your current position	Because you've excelled in the classroom for a long time, you think you could share your experience and knowledge with a team. You consider your purpose and ask if your current position fits you best. You seek answers in different places, connect online with other educators, return to school, or explore options to stay fresh.
Direct suggestion	An administrator or colleague asks you directly to consider a change. They have noticed your leadership abilities and encourage you to share those beyond the classroom.
Change in life circumstances	As we segue into different parts of our lives (particularly mid-career), our needs and desires change. It is likely you started teaching young and now you could be married or recently divorced, or you just had a child or a second child and your priorities have shifted. You still love teaching; you just don't have the same life you did when you started. For your family or for yourself, you may need to make a change for a variety of reasons. Give yourself permission to step away if you need to.

Sign	Meaning
Increase in depression or anxiety	Mental health is finally being openly discussed in education, but not nearly as much as it needs to be. Teaching is a highly taxing job (and if you're anything like me, you take it very personally) and when you aren't feeling like your best self, it is hard to give 100%; it may even be hard to give 80%. If you're struggling with anxiety or depression, I urge you to do what you need to do to feel better. For example, I have been going to therapy for most of my life, and the opportunity to talk about my concerns and struggles helps me stay even. It's not for everyone, but it has helped me.
Desire to go back to school or to continue your education to follow your passion	Perhaps you are already thinking about a career move that may involve more schooling, but going to school at night isn't going to work for your schedule. Maybe you need a sabbatical if your school system has them or maybe you need something more than that. I recommend researching to figure out the best and most cost-effective way to do the learning you need to do to pave your path forward.

Sign	Meaning
Your current place of employment no longer feels like home or maybe never has	Feeling like you are in the right place is a big help when you are an educator. If the school you are in no longer feels like home for whatever reason, listen to your gut. Being in a school or a system where the fit isn't good can really damage your experience. (I know this one from experience too.) As a matter of fact, you may tell yourself that it looks bad to move around and you may even convince yourself that staying is the best thing for your career; this may not be the truth. If you have a good reason for leaving (and a bad fit is a good reason), then I encourage you to start looking elsewhere.

If you notice any of these signs in your life, you may need to consider switching your job or your career.

Responding to the Signs

Suppose you recognize any of these signs in yourself or someone has suggested you consider a shift in your current position because you've shown leadership abilities. In that case, you need to take the necessary action. Even if you don't switch positions or schools immediately, you should consider a possible change thoroughly. Any of the following may help you make an informed decision:

- Search within your district or at local universities for leadership programs to identify what classes you'd need to take for another degree or advanced certification program. Can you take one or two classes as a non-matriculated student before you commit to a program? Read the class descriptions and ask yourself if they sound interesting.

- Stock up on recommended reading for leadership. Are you interested in or validated by what you read? Some of my favorite inspiring leadership books both in the education context and in general as well include:

Hacking Leadership: 10 Ways Great Leaders Inspire Learning That Teachers, Students, and Parents Love by Toni Sinanis and Joe Sanfilippo

The One Thing: The Surprisingly Simple Truth Behind Extraordinary Results by Gary Keller and Jay Papasan

The Fifth Discipline by Peter Senge

Change Leader: Learning to Do What Matters Most by Michael Fullan

Reframing Organizations by Lee G. Bolman and Terrence E. Deal

The Principal: Three Keys to Maximizing Impact by Michael Fullan

Leaders of Learning: How District, School, and Classroom Leaders Improve Student Achievement by Richard DuFour and Robert J. Marzano

The Art of School Leadership by Thomas R. Hoerr

Transformational Leadership in Education by James MacGregor Burns

Leading Change by John P. Kotter

Data Wise, Revised and Expanded Edition: A Step-by-Step Guide to Using Assessment Results to Improve Teaching and Learning by Kathryn Parker Boudett, Elizabeth A. City, and Richard J. Murnane

Building a Culture of Support: Strategies for School Leaders by Dominique Smith, Nancy Frey, and Douglas Fisher

Leadership for Differentiating Schools and Classrooms by Carol Ann Tomlinson and Susan M. Allan

Leadership on the Line: Staying Alive Through the Dangers of Change by Ronald A. Heifetz and Marty Linsky

Culturally Responsive Leadership in Higher Education: Promoting Access and Equity for All Students by Lori D. Patton and Ira E. Harvey

The Innovator's Mindset: Empower Learning, Unleash Talent, and Lead a Culture of Creativity by George Couros

Leaders Eat Last: Why Some Teams Pull Together and Others Don't by Simon Sinek

Learning to Lead: A Workbook on Becoming a Leader by Warren Bennis and Joan Goldsmith

- Talk "off the record" to current leadership folks you trust. Ask them about the nuts and bolts of their daily responsibilities and how they felt during their leadership transition.
- Search LinkedIn and start following or connecting with people with jobs that interest you. You'd be surprised how willing folks are to chat and share information. Later in this book, I will discuss many jobs that former educators currently do. There will be a YouTube playlist to watch those interviews.
- Participate in leadership chats on Twitter like #Satchat or #Leadup. Try to gauge the learning and experience of those currently in the position you aspire to.
- Search for potential jobs and note what intrigues you. Write your ideal job description and see if this position exists in your school or elsewhere.
- Attend a trade show or a job fair and see what else exists. There may be opportunities you aren't aware of. EdTech forums are another great way to connect with new possibilities.

- Talk to a career coach at your local career center or even the guidance counselors at your school. They may have resources that are useful in helping you narrow your search.

Finding the Right New Job

If you love to teach like I do, deciding to leave the classroom will never be easy. Even after you decide to leave, you may decide your heart still lives in the classroom. Keep in mind that no decision is permanent. You may want to go back to the classroom someday, so don't burn any bridges on your way out the door. But when you find the right position, you'll be challenged and feel rewarded by the move.

As I evaluated a potential change, I created a job description of an ideal position, including a job proposal, schedule, and responsibilities. Considering these elements of a position helped me clarify what I was looking for. I focused heavily on the strengths used in the classroom that I could carry into leadership. You may find that a hybrid position is the right decision at first, and then you can decide differently as you go.

After leaving the job I created myself in some capacity, what I learned was that sometimes making the first move makes all the other moves easier. The school I was in the longest (nine years) was the one I was most attached to. I was intricately involved in the lives of whole families since we were a small community and I often taught every child in a family. The program I taught I largely created and feared that if I left it would fall apart. From experience, I will share that you can't let those fears hold you back. Unfortunately, my program did fall apart, but now the program that is in place suits new leadership and the students in it. It was hard at first to handle this reality, but I am better for it now, looking at it in my rearview mirror.

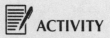 ACTIVITY

CREATE YOUR DREAM POSITION PROPOSAL

If you want to make a career move, consider creating a position proposal similar to this based on your goals and credentials. It will also help you articulate what you are looking for in a specific way. In this section, I include a school-based example and a more consultant-based option. Be creative, and don't allow what currently exists to limit your potential. The whole point of this activity is for you to brainstorm and clarify precisely what will make you happy at your current stage in your career.

Consider each of the following:

- a position title (not urgent, but it may help you stay focused)
- an overview of what the position will be used for and why it is important
- a job description
- qualifications
- job responsibilities
- location if applicable
- salary suggestions based on experience and/or market value

Remember, the more specific you get, the easier it will be to find your just-right move. You can find blank templates in the appendix so you can create your own position as well.

POSITION PROPOSAL

Overview: Proposal is for a new position to aid in teacher development, technology integration, and whole-school assessment improvement, from formative assessment creation to reflection and student empowerment. Schools considering a move to portfolio assessment and standards-based learning would be ideal.

Job title: Assessment and Accountability (Data) Coach

Job focus: Support school staff in developing assessment practices to empower students, improve learning, and aid teachers in their commitment to increase student engagement. Student-centered coaching will ensure data around student learning will drive instructional practices. Different protocols will be used to help develop student growth. Assessment and reflection practices will be embedded to ensure students and teachers learn this better.

Job description: Support the school community to build a more robust understanding of effective alternative assessment practices. Assist teachers moving away from traditional testing and grading and toward project-based learning, emphasizing formative, actionable feedback and student voice/choice. Work with teachers to design projects around curriculum aligned with standards and offer areas of differentiation, helping to include students in this process as well.

Evaluation of the position: After each marking period, the coach will look at student data, classroom practices, and teacher feedback. Administrators will be able to observe progress, discuss goals, and set benchmarks with the coach to be met over a period of time.

At the end of the year, the success of the new assessment practices will be determined by student growth and overall community buy-in. A pre- and post-staff evaluation of the new assessment practices, co-constructed with the administration, will be conducted to measure the coach's growth by measuring teachers' growth.

Qualifications

- 15+ years in the classroom as a highly effective ELA and journalism teacher
- Nationally board certified in ELA
- Teacher coach with the UFT Teacher Center
- Experience working with administrators on school committees (leadership team, curriculum, accreditation, assessment, and portfolio) to help colleagues improve pedagogy for the benefit of student learning
- Author of eight education books on the topics of alternative assessment, student-centered learning, reflection/self-assessment, questioning, homework and peer feedback, and a broader range of educational philosophy
- Blogger with *Education Week Teacher*
- Experience with technology integration in and out of the classroom
- Further credentials with my full resume and references

PORTFOLIO AND GRADING INSTRUCTIONAL COACH JOB DESCRIPTION

Location: Remote with regular site visits (hybrid)

Proposed time: July 1, 2024 to June 30, 2026 (full time, with flexible hours)

Ongoing consulting support: 26–27 school year to refine structures and train an on-site person

Salary suggestion: Negotiable with benefits

Overview: This position will oversee the full secondary implementation of the portfolio system. Working closely with the other team members, the person will ensure documents, practices, and rollout are consistent across content, grade levels, and schools. The primary focus of this position will be to support leaders and teachers with successful, sustainable, and scalable practices. This position will support site-based instructional coaches and leaders regularly working with teachers and students.

Job specifications and responsibilities
Remote responsibilities

- Template creation and revision
- Content-specific library setup and maintenance to support the work of current and new teachers
- Updating and maintaining the teacher handbook and student portions
- Collection and organization of exemplars
- Common formative and summative assessment review for alignment
- Maintaining an inventory and communication with teachers to ensure consistency and support
- Liaise between elementary and secondary initiatives for alignment and consistency
- Zoom meetings for coaching and conversations where appropriate
- Development of surveys to track quantitative and qualitative data throughout the rollout

On-site responsibilities

- Monthly school classroom visits – walkthroughs for accountability and consistency to see how things are going. Notes will give way to coaching and professional learning opportunities
- Meetings with the immediate team and other teams that the work impacts that can't be done via Zoom

- PLC visits where appropriate to review data and make instructional decisions
- Student focus groups to check the effectiveness of what we are doing. Data crunching for trends based on what is seen in the focus groups

Hybrid

- Professional learning design for teachers
- Coaching and professional learning for leaders so they can support teachers doing the work
- Support site-based instructional coaches and teams
- Provide resources to support the professional learning (strategies, articles, one pagers)
- Work with the tech team on revisions and review for collection and selection
- Work with the district communications team to ensure a coherent and consistent plan and package for internal and external sharing
- Track progress in writing a case study of the district to document the work as a model for other districts

Proposed Schedule

As part of my proposal, I created a five-day schedule with eight periods daily. You can include flexibility in alternative job periods as needed. Lunch could also be flexible. If you're looking to create a position in a school that doesn't already exist, stretch your imagination to determine what it could look like within whatever structure your current school uses. This schedule could look very different if you choose a job that isn't in a school. For example, during my regular work week now, I have complete flexibility in my time except for meetings that include other people, but I control my calendar completely.

School-Based Example Based on an Eight-Period Day

Monday	Tuesday	Wednesday	Thursday	Friday
Newspaper class (teaching period)	Newspaper class (teaching period)	Newspaper class (teaching period)	Newspaper class (teaching period)	Newspaper class (teaching period)
Teacher meetings and visitations	Teacher meetings and visitations	Teacher meetings and visitations	Teacher meetings and visitations	Teacher meetings and visitations
Teacher meetings and visitations	Teacher meetings and visitations	Teacher meetings and visitations	Teacher meetings and visitations	Teacher meetings and visitations
Co-planning	Co-planning	Co-planning	Co-planning	Co-planning
Administrative duties	Administrative duties	Administrative duties	Administrative duties	Administrative duties
Lunch	Lunch	Lunch	Lunch	Lunch
Teacher meetings and visitations	Teacher meetings and visitations	Teacher meetings and visitations	Teacher meetings and visitations	Teacher meetings and visitations
Professional Development (PD) planning and reflection time	PD planning and reflection time	PD planning and reflection time	PD planning and reflection time	PD planning and reflection time

Non-School-Based Example

(This example is different all of the time – no two days or weeks look the same.) I use both an electronic calendar and a paper calendar using color coordination. I like to use two calendars because I get notifications on the electronic one and I can see the physical one all day on my desk for convenience. You'll note that I have time in this version of my job to take care of personal responsibilities throughout the day. As long as my work gets finished by the deadline, it doesn't matter when I do it.

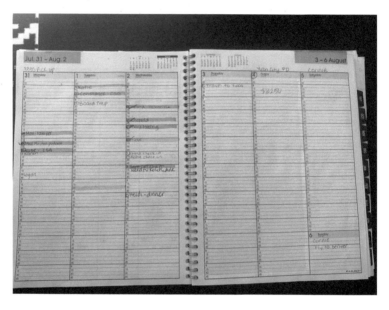

School-Based Version: Review the Proposed Responsibilities, Possible Activities, and Benefits and Outcomes

Responsibilities	Activities	Benefits and Outcomes
Teacher Model – Lab Site (This could be a newspaper class or journalism class resulting in an online student media outlet.)	• Visit teachers. • Debriefing pedagogy. • Conduct student interviews. • Share lessons and units. • Plan strategies. • Allow for teacher observations.	• Display best practices in action. • Offer a working model for teachers, outside pedagogues, and administrators to visit to view tech integration and no-grades environment.
Teacher Coach	• Target teachers in need. • Informally visit with teachers. • Provide feedback and strategies. • Assist and support teachers with tech reflection and no-grades integration. • Help develop curriculum and assessment design for the entire school.	• Help align school vision. • Help develop pedagogy. • Provide a better, streamlined environment for student learning. • Develop individual teacher voice.

Responsibilities	Activities	Benefits and Outcomes
Co-planning and Team Teaching	• Help implement strategies by pushing into classes of teachers. • Help develop student-centered activities to engage all learners. • Focus on student voice and involvement in the process.	• Support coached teachers by following through on the strategies in and out of the classroom.
Professional Learning Provider and Planner	• Poll staff regularly for areas of need. • Coordinate book groups. • Plan specialized professional development sessions for the whole school or small groups based on needs. • Plan *edcamp-style* professional development once a month to make use of staff expertise. • Teach classes on specific tech to promote project-based learning. • Promote reflection for both teachers and students.	• Ensure the needs of all teachers and learners are met. • Continue to support a wider effort to develop teaching strategies, including technology integration, to ensure enriched student learning.

Responsibilities	Activities	Benefits and Outcomes
	• Develop a schoolwide understanding of student-centered assessment and reasons for moving away from traditional grading • Promote a portfolio culture where learning is *shown through the process over time* rather than just in summative exams. • Support teachers as they help students communicate their learning better.	
Data Gathering and Analysis	• Review observations to target teachers in need. • Track the progress of teachers with student data and outcomes.	• Ensure strategies are working. • Develop plans and accountability.

By taking the time to fully realize what I wanted to do and commit it to writing, I could focus personally before making any decisions. While this specific proposal has yet to materialize, my first non-full-time teaching position was a hybrid instructional coach/teacher position similar to the one above.

Once I was clear about what I wanted to do, the aspects of my job I loved and wanted to keep growing in, and where I wanted to grow, I could articulate these in interviews. Plus, while it may seem crazy, knowing and articulating what I wanted made it available once I put it into the universe. Ultimately, the teaching/coaching position through the Teacher Center offered a new perspective and responsibilities. I still taught three classes but ran a teacher's center, taught professional development, visited teachers' classrooms, and provided feedback.

No decision involving change comes without trade-offs. Life shifts, and what you want and where you want to go often changes with it. Perhaps your building administrator suggests you take the next step or you fill in for someone in an interim position. Your path to leadership may be very different than mine. As long as you have clarity and understand that decisions aren't permanent, you can leap confidently.

Have You Been Voluntold?

Many people don't choose to be new leaders or leaders in training. Often, *their* leaders empower them or strongly suggest they move into a leadership position. Although you might be flattered if someone has suggested this, remember your career is up to *you*. No one can force you into a position you don't want. If your supervisor is a strong leader, they will know this.

Being encouraged to leap is very different than being placed in a position you didn't sign up for. If you find yourself working through a formal leadership program you feel you were forced into, take time to reflect on whether this is where you *want* to be. Passion for your career and calling is what keeps you on this path. Veering down a path that doesn't entice you the way your current position does may be a recipe for disaster. Keep your eyes and heart open. Only you can make the ultimate decision about where you end up.

This isn't only true of leadership. Perhaps you work with a vendor who sees your talents and offers to help you into a position outside of school; remember to ask the right questions and take charge of your destiny. It's your right to interview them as much as they will be looking into you.

Final Thoughts

Although there is no right time to leave the classroom or a school-based job, we all have a right to grow our careers in the way that makes the most sense for our lives at each phase. However, if you've recognized signs that your current position is stale and you aren't as inspired as much as you once were, then that may be all the information you need. If you're ready for a change, keep reading. The coming chapters will offer strategies and information to help you make the most informed decision you can.

 REFLECTION QUESTIONS

- When did you start questioning your position?
- What are the circumstances that make you want a change?
- What do you love most about your current position?
- What do you dislike about your current position?
- What are your strengths as an educator?
- What are your blind spots?
- How can you use your strengths to choose a new career path?
- Why are you most eager to try something new?

2

What Happens Next?

Seeing Opportunities in Real Time

Deciding you want to leave is potentially the hardest part. Once you've settled into the idea that you won't be returning to your classroom, it's time to manifest the multitude of possibilities that are now in your future. I know it probably sounds a little strange, but making an intention to be open to change will bring in opportunity. It will mentally prepare you for possibility and will likely help you keep your eyes open for what is to come.

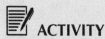 **ACTIVITY**

Take a second to set an intention for the next step of your journey. You can jot your ideas down here.

Examples: I will find an opportunity that makes good use of my writing and assessment skills. The hours will be flexible and will cover my financial needs.

I will create a webpage to market my coaching skills to invite multiple local and regional opportunities.

Your intention:

DOI: 10.4324/9781003450702-3

Taking Risks

Putting what you want into the universe will invite new opportunities. They may not be perfect at first, but you will find yourself saying yes a lot before you find the perfect fit and that's okay. When I first left the classroom, I moved into a hybrid role where I still taught a few classes but also ran the Teacher Center and provided instructional coaching and professional learning for my peers. This was exactly what I was looking for when I left the classroom; however, although it answered my initial intention, it was very far from home and it was a struggle to care for my son in an emergency. Of course, I didn't know that my son would have a bad year or that the location would be a hardship to get to when I put the intention out there; I only knew what I wanted and I got just that.

At first, I was nervous about only being in a position for a year before I left it, but the bottom line is sometimes life creates situations you have to be responsive to and those are the risks we have to take. Turns out that my concerns about my brief year at this school were unfounded. Once again, I had made an intention to get a job closer to home in a leadership capacity, and within months the next opportunity presented itself. In fact, when I took my first leadership position that was only five miles from my house, I couldn't have predicted what was to come. Up to that point, I was uncredentialed but experienced, and I went way out of my comfort zone to get the position and it paid off. This position became the basis for my book *From Teacher to Leader: Finding Your Way as a First-Time Leader without Losing Your Mind*.

Taking risks is never easy, but we will never grow unless we do. So with that in mind, we must be fearless – calculated – but fearless. As you read through this chapter and other sections of this book, consider what is possible – not just where you have already been. You need to be able to see beyond the scope of what you know and are comfortable with and stretch to places you'd like to be. Every success I have had has come as a result of a calculated risk I have taken. Some have worked out better than others, but they all helped me achieve something different, even if it wasn't always in ways I could have predicted.

To get yourself into a risk-taking posture, it is helpful to take inventory of where you are and what you want. This will aid in your ability to anticipate what your next step should be. Please bear in mind as you do this that missteps will happen – they are not just possible but inevitable. This doesn't make your risk-taking a failure; it merely sets you up for something that is even better in the future.

Taking Inventory

It's time to discover more about yourself. In the first chapter, I discussed the need to create your own job description as an exercise for clarity. While you're taking inventory, you're going to look backward to look forward. One good place to start is to dust off your resume – it may have been a while since you've looked at it and it is likely you will need to give it a refresh. And when you dust off the resume, make sure to make the necessary updates to your LinkedIn and other social profiles as well. At the very least, you will need to update it and if you know a specific job you are applying to, you can customize it to highlight specific skills that demonstrate your unique skill set and how it makes you especially qualified for the new work. If the job description exists, take the time to highlight specific attributes that align with what they are looking for. This is true for a cover letter as well.

In the image below, you will see an example of my resume and the kind of revisions I have made over the years and/or job-related revisions. The irony is as I was looking for my most up-to-date resume to share, I had about 15 versions saved for the variety of jobs I have applied to over the years and they weren't labeled very effectively, which made it hard for me to find what I was looking for. I recommend when you are doing this that you save each new document with a specific name or theme and the date of the update. I have removed my address and phone number from the document as well. One last thing to consider on your resume is your references. Add that you will share them upon request, as you can see at the bottom, but be selective about who you ask. Depending on the position you are applying for, you will need a variety of references; consider folks who can vouch for your character, work ethic, skill, relationship, etc.

Starr Sackstein
MsSackstein.com
~~address~~
(cell) ~~phone number~~; (email) MsSackstein@gmail.com
X Handle @MsSackstein

WORK HISTORY

Aug. 2021 – Present   Chief Operating Officer and partner of *Mastery Portfolio, LLC*
- Supervise and support Mastery Coaches and School Liaisons.
- Develop professional learning programs and oversee the quality of implementation.
- Provide professional learning experiences both online and in-person.
- Work with schools directly to ensure student success with SBL practices and tracking using the MasteryBook.
- Share ideas to help develop the MasteryBook tool using feedback from users to improve the tool.
- Develop systems to grow a new company in Operations.
   - Iterate on these systems to ensure efficiency.
- Oversee marketing and sales.
- Work closely with the leadership team to develop the company.

> **Formatted:** Outline numbered + Level: 2 + Numbering Style: Bullet + Aligned at: 4.44 cm + Indent at: 5.08 cm, Tab stops: Not at 1.27 cm

June 2019 – Aug. 2021   Educational Consultant and Co-Director of Professional Learning, *The Core Collaborative – I still consult with TCC now*
- Served as the Communications Director for six months through the pandemic.
- Partner with schools to provide exceptional embedded, ongoing professional learning on assessment reform using my books *Hacking Assessment, Peer Feedback in the Classroom,* and *How Do I Help Students Self-Assess?* as well as the Impact Team model by Paul Bloomberg and Barb Pitchford – other consulting work focused on curriculum development for optimal student engagement and voice.
- Strategize with schools to help bring the best learning to students.
- Developed a short, medium, and long-term plan for their social media accounts.
- Provided feedback on consultant blog posts for their blog.
- Moderate our weekly Twitter Chat #CoreChat – manage topics, moderators, and preparation.
- Oversee ongoing marketing campaigns for the company, liaising with the creative team.

June 2019 – Aug. 2021   Developmental Editor and Project Manager (announced as publisher in November 2019), *Mimi and Todd Press*

- Build systems to effectively run a small publishing house.
   - Workflow for book and workbook projects
   - Acquisitions
   - Launch of finished products
   - Research the market
- Work with the authors to ensure project flow from start to finish in the process.
- Review manuscripts and provide developmental feedback for improvement.
- Strategize for marketing and launch of the book with the communications team.
- Work with authors to develop their online presence.
- Develop a video interview program called AuthorED & InspirED to help promote authors.
- Manage contractors for interior book design and copyediting.
- Communicate and collaborate with the creative team on the look and feel of covers, interior graphics and tables, and font for projects.
- eToolkit content developer and project manager.

Sept. 2017 – June 2019   Director of Humanities, K-12, *West Hempstead Union Free School District*, **West Hempstead, NY**
- Instructional leader for the Social Studies, English, Business, World Languages, Reading, and Library departments.
- Strategic development of Humanities. This will involve liaising with the Central Office and building-level administrators.
- Be responsible, as a member of the administrative team, for promoting and developing a healthy and productive school, and useful community links.
- Be responsible as the District Director of Learning-Humanities for promoting and developing a culture of uncompromising mutual respect between teachers and students.
- Promote high expectations and facilitate the highest standards of achievement.
- Raise student achievement in the Curriculum Area by monitoring and promoting student progress and learning in liaison with the Central Office and building-level administrators.
- Lead areas of whole school development (as agreed to with the Central and building-level administrators); responsibility for priorities from Central and school goals/plans relating to the development of the curriculum and/or learning and teaching, for example.

Key Tasks:

- Support the Central Office and building-level administrators in the management of the whole school curriculum by establishing Curriculum Area policies with Humanities in line with whole school policies.
- Develop, produce, and maintain Curriculum Area documentation, including:
   - Appropriate schemes of work detailing content, method, and assessment strategies
   - Long and medium-term planning
   - Curriculum Area Development Plan and Annual Review; including action plan, responsibilities, and resource implications
   - Quality assurance-related documentation

> **Commented [1]:** I've toyed with narrowing the job description from my district leadership position, but I legitimately did all of these things. I used to think a resume should be only one page, but as my career has lengthened that is a requirement that no longer fits.

What Happens Next?

- o Record-keeping systems
- Keep the curriculum under review in light of national, local, and school developments.
- Monitor and evaluate the effectiveness of the school and Curriculum Area policies.
- Maximize the opportunities and initiatives to benefit student support and liaise with the Central Office and building-level administrators about accessing appropriate supplementary education provisions for students.
- Monitor the work of the Humanities to ensure that all members are consistently applying the policies and procedures of the Curriculum Area.
- Lead training for staff on work connected with Humanities and other whole school foci.
- Keep abreast of the latest developments in Humanities and assist with the professional development of staff within the team (for example, through appropriate delegation of work), and identify in-service training needs within the team.
- Ensure efficient administrators through regular Humanities meetings to:
  - o Promote effective communication of ideas and information among staff in the Curriculum Area
  - o Enable staff to cooperate as a team in planning, training, and solving problems
  - o Share expertise and good practice. All such meetings should have a published agenda and minutes copied for the Central Office and building-level administrators, as required.
- Manage and monitor the administrators of the Code of Conduct within Humanities to include rewards, sanctions, and celebrations of success.
- Organize the work of associate staff allocated to Humanities.
- Manage the Humanities' responsibilities in relation to assessment, recording, and reporting in line with current school policy.
- Analyze the Humanities' examination results and subsequently decide on strategies for future improvement.
- Set Humanities' targets in conjunction with the Central Office and building-level administrators and monitor progress towards achieving those targets. Ensure appropriate intervention programs are in place and monitored. To ensure student and/or class targets are set as and where appropriate.
- Be the team leader for the performance management of the Curriculum Area teachers, as designated by the Central Office and building-level administrators.
- Assist the building-level administrators in improving the quality of learning and teaching in the school. Ensuring the effectiveness of lesson plans and schemes of work, including the development of targets for the teaching and learning of content and skills within Humanities.
- Assist the building-level administrators in raising academic standards and raising attainment in Humanities across the school and within cross-curricular dimensions.
- Assist building-level administrators in ensuring that all students receive their entitlement to the full Humanities experience within a framework of equal opportunities and ensuring regular monitoring and reporting of their progress.
- Liaise with the Assistant Superintendent of Curriculum and Instruction and building-level administrators on Humanities' timetable and curriculum matters.
- Be aware of, and respond to, practice affecting the subject in elementary schools and liaise with elementary school principals regarding primary liaison.

Management of Personnel and Resources:

- Management of all Humanities resources, including the deployment of resources in the most effective way. Ensuring that appropriate stock needed for Humanities is in place. To keep stock lists and inventories up to date.
- Induct all new staff members to Humanities, and where appropriate act as a mentor to new teachers and students, in line with school policy.
- Ensure that suitable work is available for teachers covering for absent colleagues in Humanities and offer appropriate support to supply the covering teachers.
- Advise the building-level administrators on allocating classes and other timetable requirements for the subject.

Accountability

- To the Central Office and building-level administrators for the effective fulfillment of the roles and responsibilities outlined above.
- Provide information, objective advice, and support to the Central Office and building-level administrators on Curriculum Area matters to enable them to meet responsibilities for securing effective learning and teaching, high standards of achievement, efficiency, and good "value for money" and to enable them to present coherent and accurate accounts of the school's performance to a range of audiences including the DOE, NYSED, the BOE, the local community, and others.
- Assist the building-level administrators in creating and developing an organization in which all staff within the Curriculum Area recognize that they are accountable for the school's success.
- Assist the building-level administrators in ensuring that all parents are well informed about curriculum attainment and progress, can understand realistic and challenging targets for improvement, and can make a well-informed contribution to achieving them.

Aug. 2016 – Aug. 2017 UFT Teacher Center Coordinator & English Teacher *Long Island City High School,*
Long Island City, NY
- Teach an innovative 21st-century classroom that is available as a model classroom in a computer lab.
- Co-teach a dual language class that is used as a model where students are encouraged

What Happens Next?

to learn in Spanish and English at the same time.
- Prepare professional development for departments on various topics, such as: using Google docs/drive for collaboration, giving actionable feedback, using our online communications system.
- Work one on one with teachers using student-centered coaching cycles.
- Maintain a teacher resource space with different kinds of resources for all subject areas, including technology help.
- Work closely with the administration to support staff and increase pedagogy for all students.
- Participate in the PD committee, SLC leadership team, and UFT center.
- Attend regular professional development to continue growing as a pedagogue and coach.
- Assist new teachers in lesson planning, classroom management, student engagement activities, and assessment practices.

Jan. 2016 – July 2019   Social Media Manager for the ECET2 brand *New Venture Fund*, **remote worker**
- Manage the Twitter account to build the brand as the voice of @ECET2natl.
- Collaborate with the Gates Foundation staff to align social media activity with the broader Foundation initiatives.
- Promote new and existing ECET2 digital activity, such as weekly chats.
- Share social strategies to collaborate and network with other teachers to bring resources.
- Live tweet and share content from ECET2 convenings.
- Strategize to develop a plan to develop brand development on Facebook and Twitter.

> **Commented [2]:** Although this job was education adjacent and secondary, in a leadership role, it will serve me to be able to support schools trying to brand our work. It demonstrates an understanding of the growth of social media in education.

2007–2016   English & journalism teacher 9–12 *World Journalism Prep. School*, **Flushing, NY (Hybrid role as of 2015)**
- Publications coordinator for the yearbook, broadcast, and online media.
- Teacher Effectiveness team and PD Committee, implementation of Danielson Framework.
- Portfolio committee – working to help the school move toward digital portfolios to enhance student learning.
- New teacher mentor and instructional coach, working to integrate better pedagogical strategies and integration of technology for better student learning.
- Tech training for teachers in how to use online grading platforms, Google educational suite, and Twitter.
- Early adopter of Standards-based grading and implemented a gradeless classroom, teaching students to reflect and self-assess for better learning against the Common Core Learning Standards.
- Help to rewrite grading policy and a member of the Assessment Committee.
- Full Common Core and ISTE standards integration and depth of understanding for students.
- Newspaper teacher and adviser – with an emphasis on social media and online media.
- AP Literature and Composition certified – design curriculum to enhance student engagement in AP class that goes beyond the test and ensures career and college readiness.
- Student-centered and led publications and English classroom.
- Advocate for student voice through student blogging and student media
- Digital citizenship through the integration of social media in class – using Twitter to backchannel and offer extra help. Blogging and other commenting etiquette.
- AFL strategies, collaborative technological projects, data-driven instruction.
- Check out the class website at: https://sites.google.com/a/wjps.org/apliterature-wjps/ for sample of class work and student work.
- Mentor teacher and coach new teachers in the building. Help with low-inference observations and feedback to improve instruction across content areas.

> **Commented [3]:** My teaching positions support my experience and show my growth over time.

~~2005 – 2017   Online ACT scorer, *Pearson Companies*~~
- ~~Grade ACTs online holistically based on a rubric~~
- ~~Other national scoring campaigns for NC, AZ~~
- ~~Select comment codes for essays for appropriate feedback~~

> **Formatted:** No bullets or numbering

> **Commented [4]:** This whole section is likely to come out if I'm applying for a leadership role. It doesn't serve any purpose for that position.

2010 – April 2016   New York State Director for JEA *(Journalism Education Association)*, www.jea.org
- Make state journalism educators aware of this professional organization, present at conferences.
- Build and maintain a NY State journalism educators' group on Facebook.
- Liaison between educators and JEA to help build scholastic journalism programs.
- Attend and present at national conventions about topics in journalism.
- Worked on the Certification Commission from 2011–2014 – promoting and aiding in many journalism teachers getting journalism certification credentials.

> **Commented [5]:** This job, like the ones earlier in my career, doesn't support the job description I'm customizing this resume for and it doesn't represent my current beliefs about the exam I scored.

~~2013 – 2014   Independent Contractor for CUE~~
- ~~Online reviewing of educational apps, knowledge of Nexus 7 tablet & classroom connection to CCSS K-12~~
- ~~Development and improvement of forms for submission~~

> **Formatted:** No bullets or numbering

> **Commented [6]:** This position will be deleted too.

2005–2007   English Teacher 9–12, *Locust Valley H.S.*, **Locust Valley, NY**
- Newspaper adviser for *The Spectrum*, developing student-centered leadership and development of ideas through print publication and writing.
- Student-centered classroom strategies for struggling 12th-grade students and 9th-grade students.
- Creative Writing/Journalism, Writing workshops.
- Facilitator at The North Shore's Young Authors Conference.
- Collaborative projects with other teachers.
- Innovative strategies for writing and literary analysis.

> **Commented [7]:** Although this position does demonstrate early adoption of technology and being involved in cool initiatives, it is no longer relevant.

2002–2005   English Teacher 7–12, *Far Rockaway H.S.*, **Far Rockaway, NY**
- Literacy skills (reading and writing), Ramp up Program.
- Balanced literacy approach (workshop model).
- Literature analysis, peer editing, student publications (newspaper and yearbook).
- Technology team, team teaching/inclusion experience.
- School Leadership Committee/Accreditation Committee.
- School Curriculum Committee/Staff Development Committee.

What Happens Next?

EDUCATION and CERTIFICATIONS
New York State School District Leader Certification – Transitional D as of 9/12/2017
National Board Certified – 11/17/2012
Google certified teacher – 5/2014
MJE (Master Journalism Educator) issued by JEA, May 2010, renewed 2015
CJE (Certified Journalism Educator) issued by JEA, May 2009
Advanced Certification in School Leadership – SUNY New Paltz – graduated December 2018
MS in Secondary Ed in English, CUNY, Queens College – graduated with honors, June 2004
Bachelor of Arts in English, NYU – graduated with honors, May 1999
New York City licensed, New York State permanently certified

COMPUTER SKILLS
MS Office suite (Excel, Word, PowerPoint), Blogger, WordPress, Wix, Google Educational Suite, Social Media (YouTube, X, Facebook, LinkedIn, Instagram), Mac, iPad, and iPhone, Zoom proficient

OTHER NOTABLE PROJECTS AND AWARDS
ASCD Champion in Education 2022
Communications Director at the Core Collaborative
ASCD Emerging Leader 2016 – ASCD
Red Dot Cafe appearance with affiliation with TEDx San Antonio 2021
Tedx Speaker 2016 – **A Recovering Perfectionist's Journey to Give Up Grades | Starr Sackstein | TEDxYouth@BHS**
Teach100 Mentor – Teach100.com
Amazon Education Innovator – 2016
ECET2NY914 planning committee 2016
Teacher2Teacher advisory committee – Gates Foundation, 2015
Education blogger at *Education Week Teacher* – Work in Progress August 2014–July 2019
Moderator of the group Teachers Throwing out Grades with Mark Barnes on Facebook
Bammy Finalist for Secondary Educator of the Year in 2014, blogger/educational commentator – 2015
One of *Education Update*'s Educators of the Year 2012
Dow Jones News Fund's Special Recognition Newspaper Adviser 2011
Certification Commissioner for the JEA as of 2011–2014
ASNE's Reynolds Institute at Kent State Fellow 2011
Board member of NYCSPA 2010–2012, 2014–2016

Check out my LinkedIn Profile:
www.linkedin.com/in/starrsackstein

Check out my Amazon Author Page:
www.amazon.com/Starr-Sackstein/e/B00OJNVJNJ/ref=sr_tc_2_0?qid=1483481418&sr=1-2-ent

PRINT AND DIGITAL PUBLICATIONS – check out my Amazon author page
Simply May – a historical fiction novel (2009), Lulu.com
Teaching Mythology Exposed: Helping Teachers Create Visionary Classroom Perspective (2013), Lulu.com
Blogging for Educators: Writing for Professional Learning (2015), Corwin Press
Teaching Students to Self-Assess: How Do I Help Students Reflect and Grow as Learners? (2015), ASCD
Hacking Assessment: 10 Tips for Going Gradeless in a Traditional Grades School (2015), Times 10 Publications
The Power of Questioning: Opening Up the World of Student Inquiry (2015), Rowman and Littlefield
Hacking Homework (2016), Times10 Publishing – co-authored with Connie Hamilton
Peer Feedback in the Classroom: Empowering Students to be the Experts (2017), ASCD
Education Write Now: First Edition – contributor – chapter on assessment (2018), Routledge
10 Perspectives on Innovation in Education (Routledge Great Educators Series) – contributor – chapter on assessment (2018), Routledge
From Teacher to Leader: Finding Your Way as a First-Time Leader without Losing Your Mind (2019), Dave Burgess Consulting
Ungrading: Foundations, Models, Practices, Reflections – contributor (2020), West Virginia University Press
Assessing with Respect: Everyday Practices That Meet Students' Social and Emotional Needs (2021), ASCD
Hacking Learning Centers in Grades 6–12: How to Design Small-Group Instruction to Foster Active Learning, Shared Leadership, and Student Accountability co-authored with Karen Terwilliger (2021), Times 10 Publications
Hacking Assessment: 10 Tips for Going Gradeless in a Traditional Grades School: Second Edition (2022) Times 10 Publications

WEBINARS:
For the most up-to-date webinars, check out www.mssackstein.com/speaking-engagements
~~Hacking Homework – Hack Learning Series~~
~~The Power of Questioning – NFiSTE~~
~~Edchat Interactive – 7pm Hacking Assessment~~
~~ASCD webinar about Teaching students to self-assess~~
~~Wiz iQ: Teaching Students to Reflect on Personal Learning~~
~~Teachers Leading Teachers Conference – Throw out grades for better student learning~~

PODCASTS:
For the most up-to-date podcasts, check out www.mssackstein.com/assessment
~~TL Talk Radio – Season 2: Episode 13 – Hacking Assessment – Interview with Starr Sackstein [Podcast]~~
~~AJEd 020 : Starr Sackstein: Hacking Assessment~~
~~Cult of Pedagogy – Could you teach without grades?~~

What Happens Next?

Talks with Teachers - Episode 12
Nerdy Cast - Season 3, Episode 2
Wired Educator Podcast - Hacking Assessment an Interview with Starr Sackstein
Rhodenizer's Eduthoughts: Episode 7 - Starr Sackstein
Cool Cat Teacher - How to Assign Homework Without Wasting Everyone's Time
How to Eliminate Both Homework and Grades at the Same Time - Hack Learning podcast
35 Connie Hamilton and Starr Sackstein Urge you to Rethink Homework

SPEAKING ENGAGEMENTS:
For the most up-to-date engagements, check out www.mssackstein.com/speaking-engagements
ASCD Empower 18 - speaking - March 2018
Learning and the Brain Conference - speaking - November 2017
Keynote in Charlotte Schools - Assessment/Whole child - July 2017
ASCD Empower 17 - Hacking Homework with Connie Hamilton - March 2017
MassCUE and Mass ASCD Leadership Conference - keynote - March 4, 2017
What Great Educators Do Differently - West Virginia - December 9, 2016
ECET2 NY 914 - Cultivating a Calling keynote and two sessions - November 4, 2016
LIASCD - Let's throw out grades for better student learning - September 30, 2016
BLC16 - Putting Students in the Front and Eliminate Grades in the CUE tip session, Boston, MA - July 20-22, 2016
TEDxYouth@BHS - Burlington - April 30, 2016
Connected Educators Long Island, Farmingdale, NY - April 9, 2016
Keynote for the Long Island National Board Summit, Adelphi University - bringing teacher leadership outside the classroom - Feb. 4, 2016
NYSASCD - **Getting Rid of Grades for Optimal Student Learning** November 3, 2015
Edscape - Woodbridge High School, Woodbridge NJ - Oct 17, 2015 - Connected Educator Panel
EdcampLI Jericho, NY - October 3, 2015 - How to Throw Out Grades with Don Gately
ISTE in Philadelphia, PA - Poster Session on Digital Storytelling and Corwin Connected Educators Authors' panel - *Blogging for Educators* - June 30-July 1, 2015
Bronx Ed Conference at Lehman College - Teachers Throwing Out Grades- June 4, 2015
Dataeation Expo - Rethinking traditional grading- May 14, 2015
Long Island Connected Educators Summit - presented with Donald Gately on Teachers Throwing Out Grades- March 28, 2015
NBTC Teacher Leadership Conference at Adelphi University - Use Social Media to Tell Your Story- January 30, 2015
Baruch's High School Journalism Collaborative - December 2014
JEA/NSPA Fall Conference - November 2014 Twitter for Collaboration and photojournalism for CJE Certification
Edscape - Brad Currie and I will on Ed Perspectives, our On Air Google Show about teacher and administrator perspectives on issues like testing, teacher evaluations and achievement. October, 18, 2014
Speaking engagement at the Edison Township Schools with Dave Burgess in NJ - October, 11, 2014
#COL chat Call to Action - July 29, 2014
Connected Educators Long Island #CELI14 - April 5, 2014
Building Learning Communities 2013 - Boston - July 2013
JEA/NSPA Spring Conference - San Francisco - April 2013
JEA/NSPA Fall Convention - Minneapolis - November 2011
Long Island University's "Our Mutual Estate" conference - May 2011
JEA/NSPA Spring Convention - Anaheim - April 2011
JEA/NSPA Fall Convention - Kansas City - November 2010
JEA/NSPA Spring Convention - Portland - April 2010
JEA/NSPA Fall Conference - Washington DC - November 2009
NCTE Convention - Indianapolis - November 2004
NCTE Convention - San Francisco - November 2003

*References upon request

On the next page is a sample cover letter I wrote for a position as an adjunct professor at a university who is not familiar with my work. Suppose I were writing a letter for a different kind of position. In that case, I'd want to highlight different skills that demonstrate some of my other qualities or I may just reorganize this letter with similar information, using different adjectives that they have added right into their job description.

Starr Sackstein
Mssackstein.com
phone number

date

Dear Hiring Committee:

20+ years of education have taught me that perhaps pre-service teaching programs can improve. I've been fortunate to share thought space with many influential educators who have helped shape how education has changed. I'm proud to be a part of that conversation.

I am committed and passionate about mastery assessment practices as an educational practitioner. After using traditional grades in the classroom for years and being dissatisfied, I found a better way to honor all my students' dignity. Because I saw a need to help teachers, I wrote a book called *Hacking Assessment* about how I successfully put structures in place to shift my grading practices in hopes of helping others seek another way.

As a classroom teacher and department leader, I partnered with colleagues to shift their mindsets and assessment practices. In my current position as an instructional coach, I work with teacher teams to explore their assessment processes to ensure the dignity of all students. Over the past year and a half, I have worked with more than 12 schools and was successful in my ability to put processes in place and develop working relationships. I always prioritize listening to the teams to help them make hard choices and support them as they implement essential changes. With this work in mind, I can be an asset to a university community. I can be a part of a thriving academic environment and a collaborative team member to better prepare future educators and leaders for the changing education landscape.

Additionally, the best part of some of my jobs is working collaboratively with my school partners and my co-director of professional learning. We truly exploit our talents together, and that kind of working relationship is something I crave. I'm always seeking to learn more from those around me, from my network on social media, and from books I read and listen to. Moreover, I have been able to contribute to the visibility of the Core Collaborative and Mimi & Todd Press through the use of social media (developing a weekly chat to engage partners around topics that matter to us and our partners – student empowerment) and support the growth of their blog both by writing for it in a variety of formats and soliciting guest bloggers through our network. I've helped develop the pieces in preparation for publication and support of the marketing team.

I'm not afraid of a challenge, and I learn quickly – as a matter of fact, I got my leadership position without the appropriate license and learned on the fly to be the kind of leader our team needed. As the publisher of Mimi & Todd Press, I've had to implement new processes, develop a system for producing books and workbooks, and liaise with our communications and creative teams and freelance professionals. In past experiences as well as this one working for a small company and/or a small school, I've had to wear various hats to suit the team's needs at the time. During the pandemic, I took on a leadership role for the communications team despite my lack of experience. I also moved around to whatever position they needed me to help the team function better. This has also been the case with my role as the Chief Operating Officer for Mastery Portfolio – I created a team of school liaisons and mastery coaches that work together to serve schools and support each other meaningfully.

Since education relies heavily on the people in systems, being a good communicator is paramount to success. I value the people I work with and make sure they feel my commitment to their success. Working as a team is the best way for a company and/or system to thrive, and if we all have the same goals and are moving in the same direction – we're all winners.

It's with enthusiasm that I apply for a position at your university and hope that I can contribute a unique voice to the community,

Sincerely,

Starr Sackstein, NBCT
COO of Mastery Portfolio and author

Here is a second cover letter (recipients anonymized) for comparison. This one is for a Teacher Center Coordinator position. Notice how I used different information to support the specifics of the job I was trying to get. For the record, I got this job when I worked at Long Island City High School.

date

Dear Ms. Clark and Mr. Johnson:

The Teachers' Center has always held a special place in my heart as I credit its presence in my first school to my real foundational learning as a teacher. Lori Mayo led our center at Far Rockaway High School and dutifully recruited me on day one. She was instrumental in my growth as a teacher my first year and was invested in helping me succeed. It was her close tutelage that nurtured my confidence in the classroom. I will be exceptional in this capacity now, given the tools I have amassed over my 11-year tenure in the classroom.

The UFT Teaching Center is the next logical step for my career. With my great passion and skill for teaching, I am capable of helping others find their teaching voice, so they can better serve the students we teach in a meaningful way.

New teachers and emerging young career educators need nurturing. Although some things are intuitive, educating is a learned skill that everyone can use to help with. After attending years of professional development, I've actively employed the techniques I've learned immediately and often. The flexibility it has helped me obtain has made me effective in many different learning environments.

I humbly request the opportunity to interview for a position with the Teacher Center. Eagerly, I will embrace the challenge of any learning community, getting to know the student body and the staff to suit the needs of its unique environment best.

Thank you for your consideration,

Starr Sackstein, NBCT
World Journalism Preparatory School

One final thought, consider the signature you have in your email. I've seen folks with a simple title and full name and others share much other information. For example, in my signature (see page 42), I have my full name and contact, work title, website, social media handles, TEDx Talk, link to my Amazon author page, link to my calendar, and images of most of my books. I use a different font to differentiate it from the email. It is a passive way of sharing my impact in a snapshot. It is worth your time to create a signature in your email. You never know where and when folks will be looking to hire, so passive advertising isn't a bad idea.

Starr Sackstein, NBCT

Chief Operating Officer at Mastery Portfolio

Chat with me: sign up for a time

My TEDx Talk *A Recovering Perfectionist's Journey to Give up Grades*

Amazon Author page

Check out my website

Follow me on Twitter @MsSackstein

Connect with me on LinkedIn

Join me on Facebook

Where Do I Look for a New Pathway?

Sometimes when we have been in the same place for a long time, we miss the new places to look for work. For example, when I first started teaching, Monster.com was the best place to seek jobs, and now I don't think that site even offers that kind of service anymore. It also ages me to admit that I used to look for work in paper newspapers. That has changed as well. Now there are many resources to aid in your search as you go, regardless of where you are in your career. The following sections will address the varied ways you can look for new opportunities.

Job Fairs

Although we may think of job fairs as something for new professionals trying to get work, that isn't their only function. Many sectors, companies big and small, and institutions actively recruit at job fairs. At the very least, it will give you an opportunity to explore the wide array of what is available in your local market. They may also help you make key contacts if you don't find what you're looking for at first.

To learn more about local job fairs for educators and education-related positions, consider using the following resources and strategies:

- Local School District Websites: Many school districts host their own job fairs or career events. Check the websites of nearby school districts for announcements about upcoming job fairs and recruitment events.
- Educational Associations: Professional education associations, such as state-level teacher associations, may organize or promote job fairs for educators. Visit their websites or contact these associations to inquire about upcoming events.
- College and University Career Centers: If you're a recent graduate or an education student, your college or university's career center may provide information about local job fairs. They can also offer assistance with resume preparation and interview skills.
- Online Event Listings: Use online event listing websites and platforms to search for education job fairs in your area. Websites like Eventbrite, Meetup, and Facebook Events often feature local events, including job fairs.
- Local Libraries: Public libraries sometimes host job fairs or partner with community organizations to provide information about local career events. Check with your local library for announcements. Also, remember that librarians are very useful resources and they love to be of service. They are friendly and knowledgeable so don't be afraid to ask for help.
- Networking Groups: Join local education networking groups or associations, and attend their meetings and events. Networking with other educators can provide valuable information about job fairs and other career opportunities. I am going to talk more about networking a little later in the chapter.
- Social Media: Follow education-related groups, organizations, and job fair organizers on social media platforms

like LinkedIn, X, and Facebook. They often post updates and announcements about upcoming events.

- Local News Sources: Keep an eye on local newspapers, news websites, and community bulletin boards for advertisements and announcements about job fairs and career events in your area. Take a second to stop at your local grocery store or other place local folks post information on a bulletin board.
- Career and Workforce Development Centers: Local workforce development centers and career services organizations often host job fairs and offer resources for job seekers. Contact these centers directly for information on upcoming events.
- Education Conferences: Education conferences, conventions, and workshops may include job fairs as part of their programming. If you plan to attend an educational event, check if a job fair is scheduled. Some events have job opportunities even if it isn't listed as a job fair specifically.
- Community Events: Some community events and festivals may feature job fair components. While not exclusively for educators, they can provide opportunities to connect with local employers. This is especially good if you are looking to get involved locally to stay connected to the folks you once worked with at school.
- Employer Websites: Check the websites of local schools, school districts, colleges, universities, and education-related organizations. They may post information about job fairs and recruitment events they are hosting or attending.
- Job Search Engines: Use job search engines and career websites to search for local education job fairs. Many job search platforms have event sections where you can find information about upcoming fairs.

Remember to verify the event details, including the date, time, location, and registration requirements, as they may change. Additionally, prepare for the job fair by updating your resume, researching participating employers, and practicing your networking and interviewing skills. Attending local job fairs can be an excellent way to explore career opportunities in the education field and connect with potential employers. And dress to impress – this is still a first impression, even though it isn't a formal interview yet.

Internships

Usually when we think about internships, we think of unpaid work young people do in order to build up their resumes before formally entering the workplace. However, internships aren't only for young people, and they aren't always unpaid, although some may be. Like an apprenticeship, you are giving your time to gain new skills and work with professionals who can give you a formal glimpse for a specific range of time of the new work. Internships offer opportunities to try on new experiences, and even if they don't work out, you gain insight into whether or not you like the work. That being said, internships can be competitive and hard to get; but so are the jobs in that sector. Taking on an internship can provide you with just the right skills, knowledge, and connections to break into that new field. Here are some points to consider:

Consider Virtual or Remote Internships:

- Virtual or remote internships may offer flexibility and accessibility for career changers who need to balance other responsibilities.
- Explore opportunities with organizations that offer remote work options.

Target Entry-Level Positions:

- Entry-level positions, including internships, apprenticeships, and junior roles, are often suitable for career changers.
- Look for positions that require minimal experience in the new field.

Professional Development and Certifications:

- Consider pursuing relevant certifications, online courses, or professional development programs to enhance your qualifications and make you a more attractive candidate.

Volunteer or Freelance Work:

- Offer your skills and services on a volunteer or freelance basis to gain practical experience and build your portfolio in your new field.
- Non-profit organizations, startups, and small businesses may be open to volunteer assistance. From experience, I can speak here. As a COO of a small EdTech startup, we are always eager to work with professionals as there are many things that we are still learning too. Recently, we were talking to a veteran who was looking to gain some experience, and he was willing to help us test our sales script and process. These kinds of opportunities are helpful to both parties, and sometimes you can get compensated, but maybe not in the traditional way. We are thinking about offering a commission for sales, which seems like a good incentive.

Contact Career Services:

- Reach out to career services departments at colleges, universities, and local workforce development centers. They may have resources and information about internships for adult career changers. See the above section about job fairs as well for other places you might look for a connection.

Be Open to Unpaid Opportunities:

- While paid internships are ideal, consider unpaid or stipend-based internships if they provide valuable experience and networking opportunities.
- Evaluate the potential long-term benefits of the internship.

Stay Persistent and Resilient:

- Career changes can be challenging, but persistence is key. Be prepared to face rejection and keep applying for opportunities that align with your goals.

Remember that internships for career changers may not always be labeled as "internships." Some organizations may offer apprenticeships, returnship programs, or transitional roles designed for individuals making a career change. Be proactive in your job search and networking efforts to discover these opportunities and demonstrate your commitment to your new career path.

Networking Opportunities

Again, I'm sure you have thought of this already, but I'd be remiss to leave it out. Networking offers a variety of opportunities to speak with people who can either be the main contact or who can connect you to the right people for what you are looking for. Social media is a great spot to make an initial connection, but there are some non-traditional ways to make those connections.

Non-traditional networking opportunities can be valuable for building meaningful professional connections and advancing your career. These unconventional networking approaches can help you expand your network beyond the typical events and platforms. Here are some non-traditional networking opportunities to consider:

Edcamps: If you have never been to an edcamp then you are missing out. Edcamps are considered "unconferences" because they are spontaneous and hyperlocal. You can find them if you search Google or the Edcamp website. When you go to an edcamp, there is a blank board to fill in sessions. Anyone can present on any topic. You don't have to come prepared with a slide deck as the sessions are meant to be conversations. People are encouraged to go anywhere they are interested, and they are also encouraged to leave a session if it isn't something that keeps their interest. No one is offended if you leave a session. It's a great place to find local folks with similar passions and have deep conversations.

Volunteering: Volunteering for causes or organizations you are passionate about can introduce you to like-minded individuals and professionals from various backgrounds. Non-profit organizations, community service projects, and charity events are great places to volunteer and network. Like internships mentioned above, volunteering offers a multitude of additional opportunities, and you get to give back, which feels good. So if an opportunity arises to help an organization, rather than just give a donation, consider getting involved.

Online Forums and Communities: Participate in online forums, discussion boards, and social media groups related to your industry or interests. Engage in conversations, share your expertise, and connect with professionals who share your passions.

Professional Associations: Joining niche or specialized professional associations can provide access to a smaller, tight-knit community of experts and practitioners in your field. These associations often host events and conferences that facilitate networking. My favorite organizations in education have been ASCD, ISTE, JEA, the Aurora Institute, and more. Over the course of my professional career, I have been a member of many organizations – some big and some small – and they all taught me something. Beyond learning, I have made amazing relationships with people who have been supportive and helped to challenge my beliefs.

Hackathons and Coding Challenges: If you work in technology or software development or you want to, participating in hackathons, coding challenges, and open-source projects can help you collaborate with peers and showcase your skills to potential employers.

Meetups and Interest-Based Groups: Attend local meetups, clubs, and groups centered around shared hobbies, interests, or side projects. These gatherings can lead to unexpected connections and opportunities. You can find groups like this on Facebook and other social media platforms, which will put you in the right place at the right time.

Workshops and Seminars: Enroll in workshops, seminars, and short courses related to your industry or an industry you have an interest in. These events often provide opportunities to network with both instructors and fellow participants.

Alumni Associations: Join your college or university's alumni association, attend alumni events, and engage with alumni in your field. Alumni often share a common educational background, which can be a strong networking foundation.

Conferences Outside Your Field: Attend conferences or events in industries or fields different from your own. Cross-Industry networking can bring fresh perspectives and diverse connections.

LinkedIn Groups and Pulse: Explore LinkedIn groups and the Pulse platform to engage with professionals and thought leaders. Comment on articles, share insights, and connect with individuals whose content resonates with you.

Local Art and Culture Events: Attend art exhibitions, cultural festivals, and performances in your community. These events attract a diverse crowd of artists, entrepreneurs, and creative professionals. The bottom line is you don't know where or when you might meet that person who will be a springboard for your future success.

Fitness Classes and Sports Leagues: Participating in group fitness classes, sports leagues, or recreational activities can be a fun way to meet people outside your professional sphere and form friendships that may lead to professional connections.

Startup Incubators and Co-Working Spaces: Co-working spaces and startup incubators often host networking events, workshops, and pitch nights. These environments can introduce you to entrepreneurs and innovators. They have the added benefit of taking the loneliness out of working from home, which can be very isolating. Even though I'm an extroverted introvert, too much alone time doesn't help me with my creativity. I need to be around other people. To be honest, this is the part I miss most about being in schools – the people.

Book Clubs and Reading Groups: Joining a book club or reading group can lead to discussions with people from diverse backgrounds who share your love for reading and learning.

Toastmasters and Public Speaking Groups: Toastmasters clubs and public speaking groups can help you improve your communication skills while networking with professionals who value effective communication.

Alternative Networking Events: Keep an eye out for unconventional networking events, such as speed networking sessions, unconferences, and networking mixers with a unique theme or focus.

Remember that effective networking is not solely about the quantity of connections but the quality of relationships. Approach non-traditional networking opportunities with a genuine interest in others, a willingness to learn, and a desire to contribute to the community. Building meaningful connections can lead to unexpected career opportunities and personal growth. And the exciting part is you just don't know where those connections will happen, so be ready for them even in the most unlikely of spots.

It's Who You Know

Many people would argue that to break into a new position or field, you have to know someone or someone who knows someone to do that. And although it isn't necessary, it certainly helps. Don't be afraid to talk to friends and colleagues about what and who they know. It may feel like a form of nepotism to do this, but honestly it's how the world works.

When I was starting out in my writing career, I had unexpected help which made the process that much easier. I've told this story a bunch in my life, but it bears mentioning here. When one of my first books came out, I moderated #Satchat on the early career myths which were the focus of that book. While leading that Twitter chat, Peter DeWitt, the author and blogger, contacted me via direct message telling me he liked the topic and wondered if I wanted to write a post for his popular *Education Week* blog "Finding Common Ground." I was simply over the moon. After we went back and forth, he gave me a deadline, and I got him the piece earlier than he expected. This started a professional relationship that helped me get my own *Education Week* blog (which I wrote for five years until they switched the format) as well as a book in the Connected Educator series with Corwin about blogging.

When I set out to lead that chat, I had no idea who would participate or what would come of it, but it changed my professional life. Peter's generosity was also a model of how I have tried to be in my career. Regardless of where my career goes, I will always humbly take the time to help others who are starting out. That's how this book even became a thing. Educators often reach out to me asking for advice on a bunch of different topics and I'm always willing to have a conversation or talk to pre-service teachers or via email.

This is a profession of people, and we have to support each other.

Preparing for Interviews

The whole chapter up until now has been about ways to prepare for opportunities and potential places to go sniffing for them. This last little section is all about preparing for interviews once your well-received cover letter and resume have put you on the top of a candidate pile somewhere. It can be really challenging to go on a first interview after having been in the same place for a long time. It can also be discouraging if you don't get the results you want initially. To that end, I would recommend going for interviews, even if you aren't especially interested in the position, if you have the time. It's a good way to break the ice and relax about the process because you don't have much to lose in that scenario beyond the time it took to do it.

When I went for a screener interview for my district curriculum position, I was sure I had no chance to get it. I even wrote in my cover letter that I didn't have the right certification, which is why I was surprised to get the call when I did. I arrived at the district office very early (as is my way), and the woman who was being interviewed before me was waiting in the lobby too. She had so much more experience than me and I was convinced after talking to her that she was a shoo-in to get it. After I saw her leave, I gave her a thumbs up and waited to be called in. Dressed in my best business outfit, all tattoos covered up, hair down and neatly pinned – I may have even worn a little makeup – I confidently walked into the superintendent's office where I met her and the assistant sup of curriculum and instruction. Because I felt like I had no chance, I was relaxed and answered their questions honestly. It was kind of fun. By the end of the conversation, we were talking about the next steps and I was shocked to be moving on. There were many things I had to do in a flash after that first interview, but it was all worth it.

I share this story because I am usually a bit nervous in interviews and sometimes haven't done my best, shown my best, or lacked confidence. There have been jobs I didn't get (as will be the case – rejection is a part of this game, but you have to chalk it up as learning experiences). Although you may not have any influence on the outcome of your interview, you can control the following things:

● Preparation – do a little research on the company, school, or organization you are interviewing for. It goes a long way. Don't just look at their website, even though that is a good starting point. Look up the person you're meeting with on LinkedIn; see if there is any social media related to the entity or the person. Use what you learn in casual conversation or as a part of your answers. Review the job description one last time before you walk in so that you can speak directly to what they are looking for.

- Arrive early and dressed appropriately for whatever the job is for. Not all offices call for business attire – most start-ups are much more casual as a general rule of thumb. But you can figure this out from images on their website too.
- Bring materials with you – another copy of your resume and cover letter, just in case, any other materials they requested, and evidence of your qualifications like a portfolio.
- Be polite and respectful to everyone in the office, especially the secretaries if there are any. They do hard and important work and often get overlooked.
- Come prepared with questions to ask them – you are interviewing them as much as they are interviewing you and it has to be a good fit. That means you have a right to ask questions. You will learn a lot based on their responses. Plus, I think most interviewers like that kind of preparation. Make sure you don't ask about salary in the first interview – ask work-related or culture-related questions that demonstrate your research and appropriate curiosity.
- Make no assumptions, always ask.
- Make sure to ask them about the process and next steps before you leave so you know what to expect. Waiting is the worst part of this whole process, so at least you know what to expect if you ask. Then you also know when it is appropriate to reach out if you don't hear back within the timeframe they tell you about.
- Thank the interviewer(s) and shake hands on your way out. Have a firm handshake and make eye contact.
- Send a thank you note via email after you leave sharing how you appreciate their time and consideration.

Not every interview will end in an offer, but that doesn't mean it was a waste of time. Each opportunity will help you understand what you're looking for and equally as important what you aren't.

✅ Final Thoughts

You are on your way to a new career path now. You have thought about what you want and you have taken some tangible steps to get it. If you haven't done the small activities from this chapter or the first one, here are some reflection questions to consider as you continue on your path. The next chapter is going to share an overview of some career pathways that will help narrow your focus even more.

 REFLECTION QUESTIONS

- What risks are you willing to take as you make this move?
- What aren't you willing to do and why?
- Where have you sought out opportunities already? Where might you look now? (don't forget to keep track as you go).
- Who are your key, go-to people for networking and thought partnership?
- What are your non-negotiables? Where can you be flexible?

3 Career Pathways

Do you remember being in high school or college and meeting with your counselor to discuss your options? Ironically, I remember being adamantly against going into education despite all of the folks who were in the know telling me that was the direction I should go in. To be honest, in my head, I was going to be a writer and therefore didn't want to teach. It was foolhardy at the time, but ultimately I wound up in the classroom, which was the just right place for me to end up!

This chapter will serve as an overview of possibilities and the chapters that follow will go into more depth in a variety of different areas. I'm not going to arrogantly insist that I know all of the possibilities, but I assure you that many options will be shared. As a means to making these other jobs more than just descriptions, I underwent research seeking out educators who have switched careers through the use of a survey sent out on my social media channels. As a part of the survey, I asked if folks were willing to be interviewed on a recorded call so that I could provide a playlist. You can access the playlist here routledge.com/9781032585567. It was my greatest hope that I could provide a real face and story with the different jobs as well as hear other educators share their stories. It was a great honor to speak with everyone who participated and I'm hoping to keep growing the interviews. So when you get your new job and you're ready to talk about your journey, you can reach out to me for a recorded interview.

DOI: 10.4324/9781003450702-4

The Survey

When the idea for this book became more than an idea, I was daunted by what it actually meant to collect all of this information and get it into a book quickly. So I put my teacher hat on and thought about other times I have shamelessly asked my network for their expertise and how well each of those times paid off.

I will start by saying it wasn't a perfect survey. If I were doing research for a dissertation, I might have been more thoughtful about how I asked each question, but I was most eager to open a dialogue. So here is what I asked:

- Demographic information – name, email, and job title.
- Job sector – education (traditional, non-traditional, higher ed, etc.), EdTech, consulting, instructional design, business, publishing, law and policy, coaching, insurance, sales, marketing, creative, and other. I brainstormed all of the jobs I knew people in or jobs I have had, but that is why I left the "other" on there too because I knew it wasn't an exhaustive list.
- Job description.
- How would you rate your current job satisfaction on a scale of 1–5, 5 being highly satisfied and 1 not at all?
- What are some skills you have from being an educator that make you uniquely qualified for your current position?
- What new skills/content knowledge did you need to learn for your current position?
- What is your highest level of education? Did you need more education to obtain your current position? If the answer was yes, I also asked if their new employer paid for the education.
- How did you obtain your current position? (We talked about this a lot in the playlist.)
- Why and when did you choose to leave your school-based position?
- Do you still work with schools in your current position and in what capacity if you do?

- Are there any risk factors worth mentioning with the new or old job? This one was complicated and probably not worded very well as it confused folks when they filled out the survey.
- Is there any other information you'd like to share about your transition away from traditional education to your current role?
- What advice would you give an educator who is looking to leave a school-based job into a new career path?
- Are you willing to be interviewed about your work?

The Results of the Survey

In this section, I want to share some of the results as an overview. The rest of the book is really going to try to dive more deeply into what I learned from the people in the survey and other adjacent roles worth mentioning. The survey size is 72 participants – 72 thoughtful educators who saw me post the survey on Facebook, LinkedIn, and Twitter/X. It was a Google form

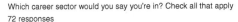

Which career sector would you say you're in? Check all that apply
72 responses

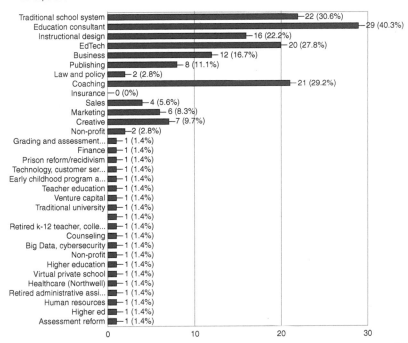

Traditional school system	22 (30.6%)
Education consultant	29 (40.3%)
Instructional design	16 (22.2%)
EdTech	20 (27.8%)
Business	12 (16.7%)
Publishing	8 (11.1%)
Law and policy	2 (2.8%)
Coaching	21 (29.2%)
Insurance	0 (0%)
Sales	4 (5.6%)
Marketing	6 (8.3%)
Creative	7 (9.7%)
Non-profit	2 (2.8%)
Grading and assessment...	1 (1.4%)
Finance	1 (1.4%)
Prison reform/recidivism	1 (1.4%)
Technology, customer ser...	1 (1.4%)
Early childhood program a...	1 (1.4%)
Teacher education	1 (1.4%)
Venture capital	1 (1.4%)
Traditional university	1 (1.4%)
	1 (1.4%)
Retired k-12 teacher, colle...	1 (1.4%)
Counseling	1 (1.4%)
Big Data, cybersecurity	1 (1.4%)
Non-profit	1 (1.4%)
Higher education	1 (1.4%)
Virtual private school	1 (1.4%)
Healthcare (Northwell)	1 (1.4%)
Retired administrative assi...	1 (1.4%)
Human resources	1 (1.4%)
Higher ed	1 (1.4%)
Assessment reform	1 (1.4%)

You'll note that the list in the previous section gave a wide variety of answers from prison reform to cybersecurity to healthcare. Some folks have similar roles and ideas, but their responses are more viable than my suggestions. You also get a sense of where educators have gone when they leave the classroom.

Here are some of the job descriptions written by the survey participants. Hopefully, as you peruse this list, you can start to see areas that interest you or that spark your curiosity. I know that I did. As you read them, highlight or star job descriptions you'd like to explore and learn more about.

Formal job: responsible to 70+ science educators annually; in charge of facilitating PLCs, running PL opportunities, and supporting teacher use of science curriculum; managing materials and budgets for new and existing courses; evaluate, select, and purchase curricular resources with teachers for schools; support instructional practices, including regular classroom visits.

Informal/non-named job: leading the subgroup of a larger grading and assessment committee facilitating the transition to a portfolio-based assessment system in secondary schools.

Generally, I provide professional development to teachers. What that looks like year to year changes with what we learn about best practices, my interests, and the educational climate.

I coach principals in a large urban district. I also provide professional learning workshops for the Danielson Framework for Teaching as well as independent consulting for schools on assessment and grading.

I support teachers, schools, and districts in the integration of great academic learning with the social and emotional skills students need to do that great work. This work takes a variety of forms: presentations/keynotes, discussion/planning groups, demonstration lessons, coaching, and more.

My job is similar to that of an assistant superintendent in a school district. I manage and supervise a manager of curriculum and a virtual technology team, 15 prison facilities, 8 principals, and about 80 teachers.

I am the co-founder and CEO of Breakout, Inc. By definition, I am responsible for developing high-quality business strategies and plans, ensuring their alignment with short-term and long-term objectives. What that really means is that I set the vision and direction for the company and helped work with an amazing team to accomplish our company goals.

Business development on behalf of the largest provider of mental and behavioral health support to schools in the United States. I work with districts to match their PD, programmatic, and staffing needs to our services.

As a partner relationship manager, I work with my company's partners/clients to ensure their satisfaction with our product. Within this role, I conduct training, collaborate on project goals, introduce new products and services, and build long-lasting and trusting relationships.

For me, "educational consultant" has meant I've done the following jobs: 1. curriculum review with a lens on reading comprehension; 2. grade reporting overhaul; 3. institution of systems for education support services; 4. institution of SEL program; 5. institution of more evolved "disciplinary" policies; 6. delivered professional development in the areas of reading comprehension, positive relationships, and SEL; 7. coached teachers, mostly around relationships; 8. wrote a book about my approach to teaching called *Joyful Learning*.

As education program manager, my focus is on supporting educators to bring Epic Games tools (Unreal Engine, Fortnite Creative, Twinmotion, RealityScan, Metahuman Creator, etc.) into secondary classrooms. We create and distribute resources that help soften the learning curve and assist with easy onboarding of our tools so that educators do not have to be an expert to provide opportunities for their students. We also offer extensive professional development for school districts, organizations, and individual educators. Our resources, training, and licensing of our products come at no cost.

Design, modify, improve, and create curriculum for synchronous and asynchronous learning for a business in order to better train and retain employees.

I do the educational testing for children with special needs or who are suspected of having a disability in order to provide them with the most appropriate support in the classroom

District-wide elementary instructional coach for a large public school district outside of NYC.

I am the content lead for 6–12 science education for Washington State.

I work with teachers to help them use technology more effectively in the classroom. I also help them with specific projects by working with students in small groups. Once a week I teach a 1st-grade class and a 3rd-grade class computer science skills.

Manage the scheduling, data, and operations around the preschool rating system of Colorado.

VP of Innovation/I develop new products and services for educators.

Operating and working with Human Restoration Project to inform, guide, and grow the progressive education movement, such as creating resources, a podcast, blogs, professional development, and hosting a yearly conference.

Prepared university students to teach secondary education.

I support people working towards health goals by instilling habits in their lives.

Operations for a seed-stage venture capital fund.

I work with fifty districts in the suburbs of New York City on all manner of curriculum, instruction, and assessment initiatives.

Teach journalism (mostly foundational level and journalism education – how to teach it). Direct the online Master's program in journalism education; direct the Center for Scholastic Journalism; direct the Ohio Scholastic Media Association.

Compose content for email, social media, and company websites to sell classroom solutions, software platforms, and textbooks to schools. Support the classroom marketing manager to create and implement email marketing campaigns to build a subscription audience.

Professor for a Master's education program, designing curriculum for culturally and linguistically diverse learners department.

Teach five classes of media production along with coordinating programming on the student community cable station seen throughout our town.

I support teachers, leaders, schools, and districts in their planning and implementation of project-based learning for students.

I help kids apply to college.

I design courses that will be delivered by a professional instructor. Splunk software can be complex, so we provide free and paid customer training. These customers are my target audience.

Blogger/consultant

Lead a small nonprofit that works with schools and systems to redesign, create, and foster school environments that are project-based, inquiry-driven, and tech-enhanced. Duties include: school redesign consulting, new school start-up consulting, grant management, client relations, and employee management.

Teach graduate courses; design curriculum; serve institutional capacity in teaching/research/scholarship.

Group/team sales, baseball consultant.

Working to further the ISTE standards and computational thinking competencies into educator practice at all levels.

I am the CEO and founder of EduSpark – a professional learning platform created by educators for educators – I am also an edtech consultant supporting schools and edtech companies globally.

I am working in HigherED as a technologist, assistive technologist, & instructional designer.

Federal program manager that supports school districts in the implementation of academic standards, provides professional development on second language instruction and provides technical assistance to school leaders to develop, implement, and maintain their language instruction educational program.

Support of our district's 1:1 initiative throughout our K-12 landscape.

Overseeing the 1 to1 program, curriculum integrations with our LMS, PD, and active role in grading policy and shift to portfolio holistic grading.

Learning experience designer.

I coach teams and schools in district alignment processes related to their professional learning communities. I also provide professional development to organizations. I run a blog and my virtual courses, too.

After a long stint in public education as a secondary and elementary teacher, a central office K-12 instructional specialist, and a school and national director with a national education non-profit, I am taking a much-needed sabbatical for a few months while I reflect on my next steps in education.

I own/operate a small business (crochet items to order & for sale) and work in ed tech for Mastery Portfolio.

The role of the CTE Pathways Coach serves as a middle school specialist to support the CTE programs and corresponding student organizations at the middle school level. Another component of this position is to curate experiential learning opportunities for students beyond the existing CTE programs of study. Additionally, it is the responsibility of the CTE Pathways Coach to develop and nurture community partnerships for the benefit of learning opportunities connected to career education.

I work to advance media literacy education through school district engagement, teacher workshops, convention programming, and virtual workshops.

I create and support learning content for my organization.

I'm developing EdTech tools and starting an outdoor accessibility non-profit while I contract online teach and develop courses.

I managed a team of 7 of my own but was part of an 80-person contact center in financial services for Northwell Health.

Heading a team that provides human-focused leadership development for education leaders.

Supporting school systems with learning and leadership.

Before retirement, I was the administrative assistant in the communications department. Duties included event planning for annual convocation, coordination of awards programs, and coordination of recognition events, including Veterans Day, Teacher of the Year, etc. Assisted department director with correspondence & social media. Made certificates for board meetings & recognition programs.

State Department of Education administrator.

Professional development on communicating student learning with schools and districts.

Instructional coach (technology + everything else) for 18 schools in the district.

I am responsible for the customer success managers, supporting NYC schools using SchoolStatus products.

I provide professional development and resources to the federal workforce.

Manage program mentors in the ELED program

CTE Pathways Coach nurtures and develops community partnerships to support learning experiences connected to career education for middle school students. This position also entails collaborating with CTE educators to support their program areas and designing and facilitating new CTE initiatives at the middle school level.

I support faculty in creating courses in learning management systems, run workshops to support faculty in using university technology, lead faculty through an online teaching certificate workshop series, and more.

I own and operate a small but growing EdTech startup on a mission to empower teachers to use power feedback- and skills-based assessment strategies. For students, this means having progress data at their fingertips so they can make their own educational decisions rather than feel like their education is happening to them. It gets students out of a points-and-averaging "gaming the system" mindset. It helps them focus on depth of learning and evidence of mastery, reflecting and incorporating feedback along the way. This, in turn, better prepares them for college and career.

Acquiring books and doing developmental edits for professional resource books.

Health advocate

Self-employed and free from filtering or alternate K-12 public school agendas.

It is hard to nail down because it encompasses so much, but summarized – designs, delivers, and supports professional learning opportunities with technology for educators and leaders. Implements learning experiences that will help them improve their practice and better meet the needs of their students.

Assessment reform, accreditation and incorporation assistance, sustainability measures, connecting schools to the international market, and coaching teachers in anything from AI to curriculum development.

After the job descriptions, they had to rate job satisfaction. You'll note that most of the folks are quite satisfied with their new jobs: only three rated their new jobs as a 1 or a 2. What we can infer from this data is that folks who leave their classroom positions for whatever reason do find happiness and job satisfaction when they shift their focus, which means you can too.

How would you rate your current job satisfaction?
72 responses

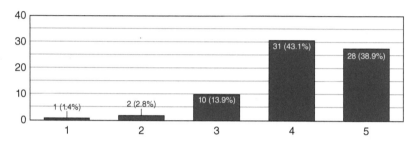

The three responses that really stood out in terms of not being satisfied were as follows. One person who is now in human resources said, "I was happier in a K-12 environment when I moved my body, interacted with kids, and laughed every single day. Now I sit at a desk and get mansplained by noneducators with "helpful suggestions" about how other people think PD should be delivered." A person who has moved into marketing said, "I don't know much about marketing. Even though it's an education company (Follett), and I was introduced to everyone as an educator (so much joy!), I am never called upon to share my opinions or expertise." And the last person is a guidance counselor who has a micromanaging principal.

In the following table, you'll see responses that speak to the skills they acquired as educators that made them qualified for this new work and the new skills, if any, they had to learn to do their new job. As you read this chart, notice trends on both sides. Can you recognize skills you have from your work or skills you'd need for specific jobs? I hope this helps build confidence as you consider your next steps.

What are some skills you have from being an educator that make you uniquely qualified for your current position?	What new skills/content knowledge did you need to learn for your current position?
Leadership, communication, technology, programming, public relations, member engagement.	Nonprofit management, marketing, board development, governance, advocacy.
Listening and presentation and the ability to speak to a group.	n/a
Flexibility, adaptability, ability to read a room, organizational skills, time management, big picture thinking (not an educator skill per se … however I was always looking beyond my four walls at the school and overall impact), interpersonal skills, computer/technology comfort.	Fiduciary management on an organizational scale (vs. departmental), navigating politics more, expanded knowledge of running PLs and PLCs, exponential growth in portfolios, standards-based assessment and grading, etc.
Organization and research. I also have to speak in front of large crowds and am very comfortable doing so.	I had to learn real estate in finance.

Educator skills that qualified you	New skills/knowledge you needed
Having experience teaching is a qualification for this position, but I've been successful because of my love of learning, listening to students and teachers, and anticipating their needs.	There's never a time that I'm not learning, even after 20 years. I started and continue to be a technology integrator, so there's always new technology to learn, but I have a passion for pedagogy. Even though I have been teaching some of the strategies and approaches for many years, there's always something new that I can learn or improve upon.
Speaking in front of large audiences, job experience as an admin that enabled me to coach admin in their work, leading school improvement work in several schools.	Primarily the product training to coach others on NWEA MAP assessments.
I have learned to work with incredibly diverse learners and to find various ways to help diverse learners thrive.	I've had to learn how to manage a business – making contacts, creating contracts, forming an LLC, etc.

Ability to overcome a fear of teaching/working "behind the wall." Fighting stereotypes about educating an incarcerated population. The major impact is that a change in governmental leadership can have on my position, my duties, and my expectations. Implementing a hybrid model of education to a population who have never even seen or used a cell phone, never mind a tablet/laptop. Being able to disconnect from the world when working at a facility (no cell phones allowed in). Patience, fortitude, and a growth mindset are of utmost importance.

Supervision, evaluation, instructional coach, public speaking, collaboration, always a teacher/educator at heart, budget experience, a visionary, and problem solver, the belief that ALL LEARNERS CAN LEARN when provided the right support and person to teach it! Flexibility, open-mindedness, and desire to see others succeed is a must. Almost forgot: tech integration.

Still in the first week on the job.

People skills, networking, music director, higher altitude thinking, marketing, calendar organization, spreadsheets, audio/video, Blue Eyes.

Educator skills that qualified you	New skills/knowledge you needed
I think being a people person, being dedicated to work, and being organized all help me in my role. I remember the creative things I would do with and for my students and fellow educators. I feel that this same dedication and understanding of how a school works and how a classroom runs has always helped me envision how practical a product would (or wouldn't) be.	I'm still learning. I have learned a ton about finance, business management, HR, spreadsheets, and data calculations, and those are not even things that are in my direct wheelhouse. I love learning new things, and even the things that I was decent or thought I was good at have greatly improved over the years. There's a lot of learning and growing in the role – and still lots more to do as time passes.
Listening. Encouraging. Support.	None.
I do quite a bit of marketing and sales. Educators are in a unique position to explain concepts clearly and address questions related to understanding. Sales and marketing do the same thing, so my education career helped me communicate more effectively in my work.	The basic concepts are the same, but the purpose is different.
Teaching/training, organization, communication skills, time management, and patience immediately come to mind.	Primary learning for this new role was product and process-related. My employer knows that those things can be taught far more easily.

Social media...ugh! Marketing...ugh! Business practices...ugh!

Developing KPIs and tracking data to demonstrate success, I have further developed my communication and collaboration skills.

1. The skill of trying and failing with equanimity; 2. the skill of trying and succeeding after failing; 3. presenting to large groups; 4. mentoring teachers; 5. deep knowledge of instructional practices; 6. deep knowledge of middle school students; 7. deep knowledge of relationship building, SEL, and the impact of positive emotions in the classroom; 8. writing; 9. creativity; 10. love constantly having to come up with new content based on the population's requirements...it's like differentiation!

My approach in the classroom was to guide my students to resources and support their learning while letting go of the need to be an expert. I have taken that idea to this position and lead from that perspective. I have also done a lot of community building as an educator, and that has been instrumental in my new position as I am actively nurturing a community of educators.

Educator skills that qualified you	New skills/knowledge you needed
Problem-solving, curriculum design, punctuality, exactness, and tenacity to understand new material quickly.	Semantics of corporate/business speak and how to network better. Microsoft products. I was a Google person.
I worked in a k/1 classroom for 14 years, so I had to learn how to turn on a dime and be flexible. I learned how to incorporate my first career into my second. I still have boundless energy and bring that to my teachers and colleagues.	Data analysis!
Building relationships and making connections. Actively listening and listening to understand. Asking questions to push thinking. Working on multiple projects at the same time and prioritizing tasks. Communicating with diverse populations.	n/a
Presentation skills, systems thinking, planning skills like travel and meetings, being able to attend to group's needs, and understanding cognitive science.	Grant administration, contracts, and purchasing.

Managing many different relationships, Microsoft Office suite, technical/quantitative acumen (was a high school math teacher).	More technical skills.
Presentation skills; passion for STEM; work ethic; creativity; ability to read a room.	Tech skills; politics.
I genuinely believe that being an educator is one of the hardest potential jobs – and what I do now is much easier. To name a few: talking with people about difficult topics, building interdisciplinary complex projects, managing a team, writing/completing applications/ grants, audio/video technology skills, and of course – the pedagogy.	Most bureaucratic stuff: 501(c)(3) paperwork, taxes, grant-writing for an organization, board policy. Or entrepreneurship specifics such as social media campaigns and financial logistics.
I understand the importance of relationships.	Most recently how best to use technology when we could not meet due to COVID.

Educator skills that qualified you	New skills/knowledge you needed
The most important is that relationships always come first. I work hard to develop relationships with people. I also use gradual release of responsibility as I coach them through the habits they are learning. I give feedback directly tied to the evidence I collect along their health journey. Also, so much of my learning around mindset as an educator comes into my work as a coach. In fact, my last client newsletter was all about a growth mindset and above-the-line thinking.	I have learned so much about nutrition & hydration – our metabolism, macros, and how exercise impacts nutrition.
Prioritizing, putting out fires, dealing with difficulties, multitasking, and project management.	Topic-based. I work with pretty cutting-edge stuff, and it's always changing.
Strong curriculum design, effective relationship-building skills, rich knowledge of education theory and practice, developed writing skillset.	A deeper understanding of central office practices, particularly in areas outside of curriculum and instruction.

Patience?

Experience in teaching, knowledge of correct form and other aspects, passion for the subject, and attention to detail – these don't sound like skills....

I had to learn copywriting (not the same as content writing) – how to survive in a business environment (different dynamics than education) – how to work in a project management landscape.

I am a writer. I worked in education. Most importantly: I was friends with the VP of Marketing.

Designing curriculum for the online space (no crayons, scissors, glue, sharpies!!).

20 years of experience in the classroom is helpful when teaching teachers – many of my professor colleagues have between 3 and 8 years in the system.

Always learning... never stops. Filmic pro camera app is my current learning project as the camera you have with you (cell phone) is the most valuable of all. Big proponent of mobile phone video production.

Supervise over 500 student video productions a year. Mostly micro but some that are massive. Learned to problem solve transforming media segments on the brink into videos worth watching. Able to capture essence of a story and visualize it with video quickly.

Educator skills that qualified you	New skills/knowledge you needed
Before retirement: loved working with students both kids and adults, enjoyed the disciplines of history and leadership which helped my teaching, researcher and author of leadership helped improve my teaching skills, long experience as teacher and principal gave me credibility with students.	See left, also critical skills included listening, humor, emotional intelligence, and love of learning, excellent mentors and colleagues, training in public speaking
Facilitation, culture building, scaffolding, meeting the needs of participants, connecting topics to other topics, connecting with people.	Salesforce, data management, marketing.
Connecting to kids.	Knowledge of the college landscape. financial aid.
Curriculum creation, conference presentations, delivery of education through multi-mode: in-person, elearning, remote virtual, hybrid. Project-based learning experience, team leadership, authoring a book, familiarity with terminology, and understanding of the environment into which I was interviewing.	Just getting familiar with business "speak."
People, writing, and presentation skills mostly.	None really, but I try to continuously improve.

Organization, flexibility, people management.

Intuitive decision-making, reflective practices, scholarly inquisitiveness.

Ability to remain calm and problem solve on the fly. Fostering positive interactions with others even in some negative situations.

Organizational skills, moving quickly without too much stress, and direct experience knowing what a teacher would want or how they might think.

Problem-solving, creative thinker, growth mindset.

Confidence in speaking, knowing the how and why behind decisions, understanding pedagogy and how educators think, solving problems from a pedagogical standpoint.

Business, grant writing/management, marketing (but I'm still terrible at that).

Corporate-type stuff like marketing and policy development; working with people who don't have the same passion; learning the landscape and politics of higher ed.

Anything related to their internal data systems and contracts.

Technical skills for software mainly, and further familiarization with applying standards/ frameworks.

How to manage different types of people, how to work with a nonprofit board, business finances.

Business and how to operate and understand business.

Educator skills that qualified you	New skills/knowledge you needed
I know the students coming into college.	Moodle and the higher ed ADA and 504 differences.
I had to juggle a lot of responsibilities when I was in the classroom as an itinerary language teacher. I had to be very organized and also learn how to respond to events and changes very quickly. Serving students from diverse backgrounds, cultures, and languages helped me be more emphatic and open-minded, and try to see the whole picture in each situation and not just from my own perspective.	I had to learn more intentionally about legislation and policy to make informed decisions and be able to provide technical assistance to educators managing a language assistance program in a school district. I had to learn about state legislation and federal guidelines for language assistance programs that I rarely needed in the classroom.
I have a background in engineering, so much of my technical/analytical expertise has served me well. Also, having a myriad of experiences in app development and coding has benefited our growth and support of classroom initiatives as well.	n/a

Honestly, my time as an educator is where I honed my educational technology skills. I have no formal training in tech, yet am viewed as an expert. I learned that right alongside my students in the classroom.

Back-end integration work, enrollment and care of devices, and purchasing decisions. Also a lot of knowledge in change leadership and district leadership with scaling projects.

Project management, design thinking, STEM and innovation, CRE, human-centered design, blended learning, liberatory design, PBL.

CRE, liberatory design, design thinking, STEM, visual thinking, storytelling for influence, leading for creativity, PBL (project-based learning).

Incredibly organized; able to manage multiple projects with ease; able to facilitate difficult conversations with team leaders; understand the dynamics of school systems to then help them overcome their challenges.

When I worked as a service center specialist, I learned high-quality ways to present PD (both in their slides or interactive elements) and also in designing a full-day workshop. That role also taught me how to create a website and market.

I'll explain my most recent position as National Director of School Leadership – teacher coaching, master board development, Title I budget management, professional development, and award-winning educator all contributed to the skills I needed in this role.

I needed to learn (for the National Director role) how to manage larger budgets, manage people, and meet the needs of diverse and C-suite stakeholders.

Educator skills that qualified you	New skills/knowledge you needed
Relating to educators is important to what I do, and the skills you develop in terms of multitasking and prioritizing/time management have allowed me to juggle the two things I'm doing.	Specifics in regards to the program I'm supporting.
I understand what it is to be a teacher, student-facing. I also understand the power of engaging students in meaningful exploration of topics of interest to them. Helping students explore their strengths and interests, and connecting those to CTE learning opportunities is so exciting to me. If a student sees school as a valuable tool for reaching their goals, then this supports wellness, for the whole child.	I am currently consuming as much information and making as many connections with members of the CTE community as I can.
Efficiency, knowledge of how to communicate, and how to teach/train.	None.
Lesson planning, curriculum mapping, time management.	Development/grant funding, program management.

Public speaking, listening, or working with diverse groups of people. Juggling multiple tasks.	Organizing and tracking longer-term and larger projects. Marketing. Doing more planning.
I am able to coach and train new or existing staff with ease. I have no worries about standing in front of 80 advisers and explaining a new process or procedure.	Healthcare and insurance-related matters.
Adaptability; purpose-driven; collaborative.	Sales; marketing.
Curriculum development. Professional learning design. Executive/leadership coaching.	Executive coaching/life coaching certification.
Excellent attention to detail, ability to confidently draft correspondence for the Director, able to successfully work with business partners in our city, understanding and ability to work with social media.	Computer programs not previously familiar with.

Educator skills that qualified you	New skills/knowledge you needed
Having the ability to balance the agendas of multiple people/groups is one skill that is a unique qualification. Being able to quickly flex from one task to another is also important. Finally, the ability to communicate effectively in all forms and adapt to changing landscapes (like changing technologies and remain current on state, national, and international trends) is critical in my work.	How to work s-l-o-w-l-y in a fast-paced world!:) Truly. It is hard to explain how difficult it has been to learn that work that can be done quickly is not done as quickly in the position/ organization where I now work due to the layers of governmental "structure" that are in place.
Knowledge about assessment, grading, and reporting. Presenting PD.	Planning extended and ongoing PD.
Organization, instructional/curriculum design, technology use and exploration, writing and communicating skills, teaching skills, leadership skills.	Some different curriculums; deeper technology knowledge helps (i.e. Google trainer/coach, MIEExpert/Master Trainer).
I am able to apply our tools to the specific needs of NYC schools.	Finance, legal, security & privacy rules, development cycles.
Curriculum development and instructional design.	ADDIE: Analyze, Design, Develop, Implement, and Evaluate. It is an instructional design model that has withstood the test of time and use.

Customer service skills, adult learning, and online learning skills.

I am new to the ins and outs of CTE and the role of a central office administrator. It's a transition into the routines, methods, information, and expectations of a new corner of public education. My previous relationships with colleagues are also adjusting to this new role.

13 years of classroom experience, coaching, data analysis.

My deep understanding of middle school-aged students, along with my experience in developing and facilitating student-directed learning experiences are a great fit for the career and technical education world. Helping students discover more about their strengths and interests and explore what their future might look like is so exciting. My background in coaching and mentoring is proving valuable in working with CTE teachers as they grow their programs and set goals. Finally, I am a networker at heart. This position requires those skills to foster community relationships and partnerships that greatly impact extended learning opportunities for students to explore career pathways. Ultimately, my teaching career has prepared me greatly.

Educator skills that qualified you	New skills/knowledge you needed
A clear ability to apply the skills teachers have: creating lesson plans, writing learning objectives, backward course design, etc. Faculty are experts in their course content but not necessarily in teaching and learning.	Just technology-specific skills. I had never created courses in Canvas or Blackboard. I had never heard of the Quality Matters rubric.
Being organized, long-term planning, giving clear directions, managing many people at once, managing time and materials, being thrifty and finding ways to do things for cheap or free, empathizing, leadership, structuring meetings effectively, creating presentations and attractive documents, having patience, learning new skills quickly and well... what can't a teacher do? We almost exclusively hire teachers because they are best equipped to quickly get good at any job.	Sales, marketing, how to connect/relate to superintendents, accounting methods, Excel, legal, how investment in tech companies works, health insurance, HR, contracting, how to become a vendor/send a purchase order to a government institution.
Understanding school, interpersonal communication, flexibility.	Publishing procedures.
Communicate well with children and adults.	Film techniques, editing, storytelling, research.

Wordsmith, knowledge, ability to create systems, actualizing projects.

Videography, technical production, marketing.

Professional development has always been something I feel strongly about – I am a lifelong learner, so I dive into anything and everything relevant. With the rise in technological uses for the classroom, there is so much to explore. Our district was part of a pilot program for micro-credentials that changed the trajectory of my professional learning experiences. From that exposure, I remain curious, a critical thinker, a forward-thinking problem solver, and willing to explore new ideas.

How to provide authentic feedback for educators/leaders.
Creating a connecting point of community for learners in a virtual setting.
Exploring new edtech resources, tools, and strategies to implement with educators.
Obtaining certifications from Apple, Google, and Microsoft (those were not demanded, however – I wanted to learn them).

I have a broad knowledge base. I am well grounded in practical rather than theoretical solutions. My network from working for 25 years in schools gives me tremendous resources to draw on.

Marketing, Salesforce, and new AI tools daily

The next few graphs have to do with levels of education. This was important because not everyone has the time or money to get more education when they are switching careers or jobs. 62.5% of educators who responded have a master's degree, and 75% of the folks who responded did not need any further education in their new positions. And 7.7% of those who needed to get more education were fortunate enough to have their employer pay for it.

What is your highest level of education?
72 responses

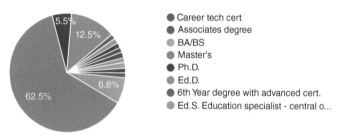

- Career tech cert
- Associates degree
- BA/BS
- Master's
- Ph.D.
- Ed.D.
- 6th Year degree with advanced cert.
- Ed.S. Education specialist - central o...

Did you need more education to obtain your current position?
72 responses

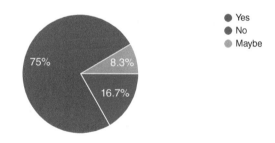

- Yes
- No
- Maybe

Did your current employer pay for your education if more schooling was required?
65 responses

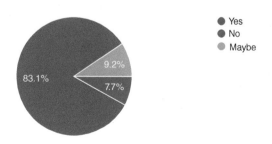

- Yes
- No
- Maybe

I'm sure you're curious about how these folks obtained their new positions, so here are the responses from the survey participants. Note that all of these methods were shared in the last chapter. As you comb through this list of gems, you'll note that some respondents created their own pathways, as I suggested in the first chapter. A few even started multiple companies to solve problems they or others were facing. Do you know a problem you'd like to solve that doesn't have a good solution yet? That's the narrative of the CEO and Founder of my company, too – there wasn't a good tool for tracking mastery data, so she helped to create one.

How did you obtain your current position?

Responded to a job posting by ASCD for a director of constituent services.

Self-employed.

Already in-district, interviewed for the position when it opened.

After I left teaching, I took the necessary coursework. I spent some time as an appraiser's assistant and then worked for other appraisers. Then, I chose to open up my own company.

I was working in a Catholic school and not making very much money, but even more than that, I disagreed on pedagogy practices with my principal and was looking for a new opportunity. This position came up at a time when jobs were few and far between, and it paid triple the salary so I thought I'd give it one year and then get back to the classroom.

Referral from a friend who worked at NWEA.

I struck out on my consulting work after I realized I was no longer aligned philosophically with the non-profit organization I was working for.

I saw the posting on LinkedIn.

---

3 years of self-motivation and a ton of hustle ... and LinkedIn.

I co-founded the company I work in. My previous roles in Edtech were also created when I founded the company (eduTecher, eduClipper, WeLearnedIt, eduGames).

I was approached by a recruiter. I have held a handful of positions since leaving education.

Found on LinkedIn and went for it.

I declared myself a consultant after I left my teaching job. So far, so good.

I started as a contractor with Epic Games after applying for a mega grant and getting the attention of the education team. I worked for about a year developing lesson plans for other educators to use to support implementation of the tools. It was a natural progression as my hiring manager was interested in bringing me on full-time based on our work together and the need to grow the secondary education program.

LinkedIn.

I became an instructional reading coach through a NYC mayors initiative within the NYC DOE; I was able to apply to be a district-wide instructional coach with a Long Island school district after four years.

I applied. But I also knew people at the state agency from some of my leadership work.

The position at my school was open the year before and not filled. I let my building principal know I wanted to apply for it. I also began taking courses for that position. Since we get money for coursework through our teacher contracts, I used that to help pay for half of my coursework to earn my endorsement.

Saw a position, and applied for it, but then I interviewed for the manager position and got that.

I worked with the President at a previous company

My employer paid for my education and schooling, but it wasn't related to my current career path. After working part-time at HRP for years, I obtained my position, eventually finding grant funding that awarded funding for full-time status.

Recruited based on perceived leadership in the field. Then interviews, teaching demonstrations, and administrative approval.

I was a client first.

By accident. I reconnected with a friend, now also my boss, and began helping with projects without expectation of pay – because that's what teachers do. He paid me, referred me to my first job in an edtech startup, and now I'm full-time with him only.

Traditional interview structure.

Worked my way up from almost a gig position, building the high school connection, getting donations and doing projects to bring in $.

I was friends with the VP of Marketing. I emailed her and asked if she had openings, and she did. I still went through the interview process and wasn't hired based on our friendship. There was excitement over my teaching experience as well as my writing test.

I started consulting and then they asked me to join full-time

Serendipity.

I was with the company on a part-time basis and went through the interview process for full-time.

Applying through the open market.

LinkedIn Premium was my main source of jobs. After 4 interviews it was offered. I did notice an increase in big company response towards the end of the year. Smaller companies I did not see any difference.

I took my pension and reinvented myself

I started a new job profit as the executive director.

Luck. I entered my institution in one role, and quickly they saw value in my work and moved me into a different position. It took a good leader with a keen eye for people to know what was happening.

Friend.

LinkedIn job posting.

I founded the school.

Founded my own company.

Newspaper ad.

I applied through the state job opportunities website that includes job postings for all state agencies. I had in-person interviews and then received an offer.

I applied for a vacant position and was offered the position following an interview process.

While working in the library I oversaw a transition to it being a media center. From there, I developed one of the first online courses offered for original credit by traditional public schools in the state. During that time I was able to act as a media specialist and worked on my adult ed theory. I then applied for the technology coach position in my current district.

I was a substitute teacher for a year before becoming a full-time classroom teacher.

After publishing our first book, we had the demand to work with teams independent of my specialist work.

I received a promotion after two years of being a successful director of school leadership.

Indeed application.

I was asked to apply for it.

Networking.

Online application.

Startup Weekend as the event that kick-started it. Then it was just my interest in running my own business. I am now doing contract work with a school to make some side money as I build new things. That paying job was through my education connections as a full-time teacher.

Through networking with a former colleague at another company.

Connections.

Networking.

Book publication.

Submitted application when moved to this area.

I applied and was the successful candidate after a competitive interview process.

By retiring from the school district.

Advertised in our current district. Applied and was one of 2 people hired for brand new coaching positions. I had built up lots of skills and experiences (technology, curriculum, etc.) over time that made me a very good candidate for this position.

Knew people in the company.

Learned the federal resume process, and repeatedly applied for many years.

Referral.

I was asked to apply for the position.

I found the posting on the university job board.

I created it out of thin air. In seriousness, I recruited two business partners, and we started the company together, building our initial product before hiring other team members as we grew. We raised an initial $350,000 to be able to give up other jobs and work on the project full-time. That funding lasted us four years and was augmented by our revenue (over $250,000 to date), but there have been times that we've had to pay ourselves little or nothing as cash flow in an EdTech business can be a challenge.

Applied after the publisher reached out on Twitter.

I created it.

Followed my passion.

I started part-time while I was still a classroom educator. This was the company I mentioned before that had provided our PD for our school + I reached out and asked if they needed anyone to support or assist with micro-credential creation/submissions. I was so impressed with their personalized approach to giving feedback for evidence submitted for contact hours. It blew me away.

Took a one-year sabbatical to try different options and network. Patience is key.

Even though the respondents left the classroom and some left schools altogether, 75% still work with schools in some capacity. Whether it is solving a problem educators have or instructional or leadership coaching, many have remained connected in meaningful ways. In the conversations I had with the educators for the playlist, many of us discussed the possibility of going back to the classroom in the future.

Did you still work with schools in your current position?
72 responses

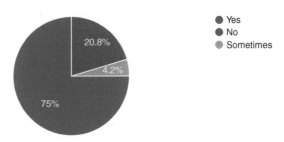

- ● Yes
- ● No
- ● Sometimes

20.8%

4.2%

75%

Additional Comments, Risk Factors, and Advice

To close out the survey data, I will highlight some of the additional feedback folks wanted to share, their advice, and potential risk factors. As I read all of this, most of it resonated with me and echoed the thoughts and fears I had myself when I was ready to leap away from my first education home, the classroom. Rather than give commentary on why I chose what I did, I'm going to let their statements stand on their own, as a chorus of support for whatever you decide to do.

 Some Additional Comment Highlights

"I think many teachers, including myself, find joy in the direct impact that we have on students and that can be hard when you leave the classroom. I now view it as reaching teachers across the state if not nationally, and those teachers impact their students. Even though I don't get the rush of being witness to student success all the time, I do get it sometimes and know that I am having an indirect impact but on a much larger scale."

"I've had substantially more time to pursue personal projects and passions while not working in a school, which was a pleasant bonus!"

"I get asked all the time if I miss the kids. The honest answer is that I do. I loved the relationships I built with my students and my colleagues in the school setting. You spend so much time with them and it is very rewarding work. That said, I don't miss some of the constraints and structure and busy work that comes with it. I am more busy than I have ever been before and work harder and longer than I have before – but it feels worth it in a different way as I help pave my own path."

"I have found that corporate America better realizes and appreciates the skills, talents, and abilities of educators than the traditional educational system does. A motivated educator can do quite well in the corporate world."

"Do NOT burn your bridges when you leave! A graceful exit leaves opportunities open and strong relationships."

"It was so difficult and it is NEVER about the students! I had a great opportunity and I was tired of battling my district to be more equitable and innovative."

"My new position has been a perfect blend of working with students and teachers. It was the perfect move for me! I still work with students, and I can advocate for teachers at the same time."

"Despite the risks of self-employment, I am so happy in my new role. I wrote a book! It was the culmination of a lifelong dream to do that. And I love teaching teachers. I still get that same thrill of "they got it!" when I'm dealing with adults. It's very rewarding."

"I miss working with kids! If teachers were more supported, had more scholarship and means to further the profession, and were paid adequately – not only would I still be teaching but HRP likely wouldn't need to exist."

"I think stepping away from traditional educational roles is a leap of faith. It doesn't work out for everyone, yet the people who really recognize the skills they have as educators see that those skills are so useful elsewhere. I hate to see talented people leave education, but I also know that being stuck in one job all one's life isn't the norm."

"I created a community of practice for classroom teachers, and I believe this was my way to stay connected to students and continue learning. If we love the classroom but want to follow another path, we might still find ways to stay connected."

"On my last day of teaching, an AP who was new to the school asked me if I'd ever considered teaching adults. I wasn't sure what he meant by that until I started my next job at a global corp at a very entry-level position and was told within 3 months that I was being fast-tracked to a supervisor because of my ability to lead and coach people."

 *Risk Factors*

"Ha! All the risks I mentioned above. Starting a high-growth company is not for the faint of heart. It takes a certain constitution where you have to be decisive, but you also don't look back with regret on poor decisions made, and take credit for good decisions made, as that's the wind in your sails that will keep you going. It takes an almost arrogant level of confidence to be a bold CEO and create something out of nothing. (One of the reasons I'm not the best at it.)"

"For me, it was different, so big learning curve plus working from home isn't fair for everyone."

"There is always the risk of litigation or being named as a party in litigation if the district or department is sued. Also, I do not discuss my outside consulting, teaching, or investigative work so there is no co-mingling or mis-understanding of the roles. I always take leave if any outside work overlaps with departmental work time to ensure a clear separation of time and roles. There is an additional risk that others may wish to do outside work and are not tapped for the kind of work I'm doing, making what I do threatening to them in some way."

"Feels less reliable than teaching as you can get laid off at any time, not just end of the school year. Keep your teaching license renewed as a backup (I swore I would never need it again until I needed it)."

"COVID."

"Personal safety is probably the largest risk factor. Being an adult in a high school around students that you don't have a relationship with increases the chance that you can endure verbal or physical harassment or harm."

"I have very little job security, but manage my money to make sure I have glide paths to different work if I need it."

"Economic risks more intense in the last few years."

"There is a constant threat of both virtual and physical danger in schools, especially in conservative areas: whether it be "doxxing" and claiming that one is a Marxist, socialist, etc. which can lead to actual physical harm; or constant mental health issues of overworking, stress, and lack of support from buildings to build a better education system. My new job has an element of that, but because it isn't within a public school it doesn't have the same vibes."

 Advice and Encouragement

"Start planning a new career while you're still teaching. Make lots of connections and think about how to get a new job before you leave. It's hard/humbling landing a new career."

"Don't limit yourself to edtech. Define the skills you have. Get a professional to help you with translating the relevant experiences that translate. But keep in mind that some of what you did in education is not relevant. Monitoring the hallways during lunch should not go on the resume. But things which do are: creating something from scratch, leading a team, reaching out into the community, doing something unique that had a direct impact, presenting ideas to a group of people, writing articles that are published, and did you do something that is considered not-status-quo?"

"Be careful. You do not realize what you lose when you leave the classroom until you are already gone."

"You have so many more skills and qualifications than you realize. And you are still able to impact students and teachers in a positive way from outside of schools... sometimes even more so than when you are in the classroom."

"You can do it. Have the courage and have a plan. Don't be afraid to take the risk."

"You have plenty of transferable skills. When you feel your time has come to an end, find something that will light your spark once again. Being an educator should be rewarding and fulfilling."

"Follow your passion and be willing to take a risk and bet on yourself."

"Explore your options before taking the leap. There are many different opportunities from writing, to business, to marketing, customer service, and sales."

"Thoroughly explore the possibilities and go through some exercises that help you understand your values, your character strengths, and how you find meaning and purpose. I think when you fully understand these areas, it helps guide you to a path on which you can flourish."

"Don't rush into it. Wait until the fit seems natural and appropriate. Many people ask me about it as if I simply started applying for jobs while the truth is that this was many years in the making and not something I was necessarily looking for."

"Leverage the skills of being an educator toward related domains. Personally, I found the transition out of education to be easy into non-profit work since it's still about "changing the world" – I wasn't losing a greater purpose to just make more money (in fact, I make about the same amount). Finding jobs that relate to education (or saving the planet more broadly) keeps the passion alive that initially was stoked in being a classroom teacher."

"STAY for at least 5 years! If you are thinking of leaving, try another school!"

"Follow your heart. It works out for those who aren't afraid to work."

"You need to have confidence. If you need someone else to convince you to own your own educational consulting company, you shouldn't do it. If you do not believe in your ability and the need for what you will offer, I don't believe the opportunities will present."

"Know that for the most part, you can always go back. Success isn't defined by only doing the same thing your whole life, so if you feel like other journeys sound interesting, know that you don't need anyone's permission."

✅ Final Thoughts

Reading through the survey results was really a catalyst for so much more of the research that went into the rest of the book. Not only the categories and sectors mentioned, but the thoughtful responses helped humanize this process. When a person is considering leaving a profession that is considered a calling, it can feel lonely and destabilizing. Being an educator creates routine and consistency and walking away from that is not an easy decision. Many of the folks involved in this survey left because of COVID-19, but others left for different reasons. Whatever your reason is, it is valid for you and don't let anyone tell you otherwise.

Chapters 4 through 10 are very much a "Choose Your Own Adventure" experience. If you have a particular interest in an area or you are curious about something specific, don't feel a need to read them in order. Read them as you need them.

Then come back to Chapter 11 and start thinking about your legacy.

 REFLECTION QUESTIONS

- What trends did you notice as you sifted through the data?
- Which job descriptions sounded like a good fit and why?
- What are you curious about as you head through the rest of this book and into your job search?
- What kinds of fears are you experiencing and why?
- How will you use what you have learned in this chapter to make some initial decisions or a plan?

4   More Education?

Now that you are actively looking for your new career path or next job, you may ask yourself, "Do I need more education to do this successfully?" To be honest, I'm always looking for a good excuse to go back to school, but that isn't how everyone looks at it. Likely, you won't need a new degree for this new career path or job, but that doesn't mean you can't go out of your way to brush up on some skills you practice or learn more about online for free.

It has always baffled me that many educators don't take their continuing education as seriously as they should. Since we work in education and there is always research and more tools to incorporate into what we do, I have found it essential to stay on top of my professional learning regardless of my role. Whether you enroll in a typical degree or non-degree program at an in-person school or online or sign up for webinars and/or participate in online chats, staying in the know is important. Additionally, being up to date and/or having opinions about the latest tools can only assist in your job search, as many interviews may include questions about these changes.

Do I Need Another Degree?

Deciding if more school is necessary can be an arduous decision, as where you are in your life dictates how much time you have to dedicate to spending more money on education.

DOI: 10.4324/9781003450702-5

Fortunately, some employers will help offset the cost if the degree is required to do the work. Ironically, this is a decision I've struggled with for years now. When I was in my mid-20s, I was certain I wanted a Ph.D. in urban planning and policy to support the students I was working with at the time and their families. As I applied for the programs, life happened, and I found out I was pregnant. Over the years, I've repeatedly considered returning for it and have always been thwarted. So, instead, I went for National Board Certification in the classroom and got my admin certification as well. Fortunately, I finished paying off the loan for the certification just in time for my son to go to college, and I got a grant to pay for National Board Certification.

Recently, I learned there is a way to achieve a Ph.D. by publication, which is now a route I may consider. The jury is still out on my journey, but each of us has our own decisions to make about whether and when to pursue higher education or certification.

Ph.D. or Ed.D.?

As I mentioned above, I have wrestled with this decision; depending on who I ask, either is acceptable depending on the purpose of getting it. When I was in my education leadership program, my law professor insisted that a Ph.D. was more respected in the field, and if I was going to spend the time getting another degree, this is the one that would get me the prestige needed to move ahead. She also said it would provide the kind of rigor I find inspiring. Other friends who have gone through Ed.D. programs insist this is the best option for practitioners. However, many in academia don't recognize the Ed.D. as equivalent to a Ph.D.

An Ed.D. (Doctor of Education) and a Ph.D. (Doctor of Philosophy) are both doctoral degrees, but they have different focuses, purposes, and career outcomes. The choice between pursuing an Ed.D. or a Ph.D. in education often depends on an individual's career goals and interests. Here are the key differences and factors to consider:

Ed.D. – Doctor of Education

Focus: The Ed.D. is typically a professional doctorate with a practical focus on educational practice, leadership, and administration. It is designed for educators and administrators who want to enhance their leadership and management skills in educational settings.

Research: While Ed.D. programs include research components, the research tends to be applied and practice oriented. Ed.D. candidates often conduct research projects on solving real-world educational problems or improving educational systems.

Ph.D. – Doctor of Philosophy

Focus: The Ph.D. in education emphasizes research, theory, and scholarly inquiry. It is designed for individuals interested in conducting original research and contributing to the field's theoretical and empirical knowledge.

Research: Ph.D. programs strongly emphasize conducting rigorous, independent research that advances the field of education. Ph.D. candidates typically work on a substantial dissertation that contributes new knowledge to the discipline.

Ed.D. – Doctor of Education

Dissertation: Instead of a traditional Ph.D. dissertation, Ed.D. programs often require a doctoral project, typically a practical research study or a capstone project that addresses a specific issue in education. Some institutions are also shifting to capstone projects that address a problem of practice (PoP) with immersion. Baylor University has an example of this. You can learn more about this here: https://onlinegrad.baylor.edu/edd/pop-and-immersion/

Career Outcomes: Ed.D. graduates often pursue leadership roles in educational institutions, such as school principals, superintendents, higher education administrators, curriculum developers, or instructional designers. The degree is well suited for those who want to impact education policy and practice directly.

Duration: Ed.D. programs may be shorter than Ph.D. programs, as they often focus more on coursework and practical experience.

Ph.D. – Doctor of Philosophy

Dissertation: The Ph.D. dissertation is an original piece of research that significantly contributes to the field. It often involves deeply exploring a specific research question, theory development, or empirical study.

Career Outcomes: Ph.D. graduates often pursue academic careers as professors or researchers. They may also work in research institutions, government agencies, or organizations where strong research and analytical skills are valued.

Duration: Ph.D. programs are longer and more research intensive, often requiring several years.

More Education?

Factors to Consider When Choosing Between an Ed.D. and Ph.D. in Education:

1 Career Goals: Consider your long-term career goals. An Ed.D. may be a better fit if you aspire to be an educational leader, administrator, or practitioner focused on improving educational practice. A Ph.D. may be more suitable if you're interested in conducting research, teaching at the university level, or pursuing a career in education research.
2 Research Interests: Assess your research interests. If you strongly desire to conduct in-depth research, develop new theories, and contribute to the academic discourse in education, a Ph.D. program may align better with your aspirations.
3 Practical Experience: Ed.D. programs often emphasize practical experience and leadership development. An Ed.D. may appeal more if you value hands-on experience and want to apply your knowledge directly in educational settings.
4 Time Commitment: Consider the time commitment required for each degree. Ph.D. programs are typically longer and more research intensive, while Ed.D. programs may offer a quicker path to completion.
5 Financial Considerations: Evaluate the costs associated with each program, including tuition, fees, and potential financial support or scholarships. Additionally, consider the potential return on investment regarding career advancement and earning potential.

Choosing an Ed.D. or a Ph.D. in education should align with your personal and professional goals. Both degrees can lead to fulfilling careers in education, but they have distinct focuses and outcomes that cater to different career paths and interests within the field of education. It's a good idea to find the right program. If you know colleagues, friends, or family members who have sought higher education, talking to them about their experiences may help you weigh their pros and cons.

Certifications

Educators can pursue various certifications and credentials to enhance their marketability, expand their skill set, and advance their careers in education. The specific certifications you should consider will depend on your area of expertise, career goals, and the grade level or subject matter you teach. Here are some certifications and credentials that can make educators more marketable. Remember that every state requires different qualifications, so if you switch markets, check ahead for what you need.

- **Teaching Certification/License**: If you're not already certified, obtaining a teaching certification or license is essential for most teaching positions in public K-12 schools. The requirements vary by state, but it typically involves completing a teacher preparation program and passing relevant exams and, in some cases, doing observation hours or student teaching.
- **National Board Certification**: Offered by the National Board for Professional Teaching Standards (NBPTS), National Board Certification is a prestigious credential for teachers who have demonstrated advanced teaching knowledge and skills. Achieving this certification can lead to increased career opportunities and higher salaries. I found the National Board process career altering, and I learned more about myself going through the process than I ever did from observational feedback from my administrators. I strongly recommend National Board Certification if you are determined to stay in the classroom but are looking for a meaningful and practical challenge.
- **Subject-Specific Endorsements**: Obtaining endorsements or additional certifications in specific subjects, such as special education, ESL (English as a Second Language), or STEM (Science, Technology, Engineering, and Mathematics) can make you more marketable for positions in those areas.
- **ESL/TEFL Certification**: For educators interested in teaching ESL (English as a Second Language) or English to

speakers of other languages, obtaining a TEFL (Teaching English as a Foreign Language) or TESOL (Teaching English to Speakers of Other Languages) certification can be valuable, especially for international teaching positions.

- **Educational Leadership Certificates**: If you're interested in educational leadership roles, consider pursuing administrative certifications like Principal Certification or School Administrator Certification. These credentials are often required for principal, vice principal, or superintendent positions.
- **Special Education Certifications**: Special education certifications, such as Special Education Teacher Certification or Board Certified Behavior Analyst (BCBA) certification, can enhance your qualifications for working with students with disabilities.
- **Advanced Degrees**: Earning a master's or doctoral degree in education or a related field can significantly boost your marketability and open up higher-level positions, such as educational leadership roles, curriculum development, or educational research.
- **Technology Integration Certifications**: As technology plays an increasingly significant role in education, certifications related to technology integration, such as Google for Education Certified Educator or Microsoft Certified Educator, can be advantageous.
- **Career and Technical Education (CTE) Certification**: CTE certifications are essential for educators specializing in vocational or career-focused programs, including automotive technology, culinary arts, and healthcare.
- **Reading Specialist Certification**: For educators interested in literacy and reading instruction, obtaining a Reading Specialist Certification or Literacy Coach Certification can enhance your ability to support students' reading and literacy development.
- **Online Teaching Certifications**: As online and blended learning opportunities expand, certifications related to online teaching and instructional design, such as the Quality Matters (QM) Certification, can be beneficial.

- **Early Childhood Education Certifications**: Certifications in Early Childhood Education or Pre-K teaching can be valuable for educators working with young children.
- **Advanced Placement (AP) Certification**: If you teach AP courses, earning certification as an AP teacher can demonstrate your expertise in delivering high-level coursework.
- **Dual-Language or Bilingual Certifications**: Bilingual educators can pursue certifications demonstrating their proficiency in teaching multiple languages. This kind of certification can help get a job in an immersion program or a dual-language program.
- **Cultural Competency Training**: Certifications or courses in cultural competency and diversity can be valuable for educators in today's diverse classrooms. DEI (diversity, equity, and inclusion) is an area of great focus now, and getting training in it can be helpful regardless of what career path you choose from here.

When considering certifications, it's essential to align your choices with your career goals, the needs of your students, and the demands of the education field in your region. Additionally, staying up to date with continuing education and professional development opportunities can enhance your marketability as an educator.

Final Thoughts

Deciding to enroll for more education is never an easy decision, especially in a middle to later career, as it is likely that you are already balancing your outside life with your job. Should you decide to get involved with more learning, many avenues can support you. Although this chapter has a list to help with some options, other alternatives exist in specific states and other countries. For example, I recently learned about an alternative route for a Ph.D. using my past publications as a means to that end. You need to stay in dialogue with folks who have gone through this process and work with higher education and possibly even state education departments. Sometimes you can get grants to offset the cost of more schooling if cost is a concern. There are also many free options if you want a deeper understanding.

REFLECTION QUESTIONS

- What research have you done regarding what is needed to do your future job?
- Who have you spoken with to validate the research you have done?
- Have you looked into specific programs? What are the pros and cons of the programs you have researched?
- If you have considered another degree, what are some of the obstacles holding you back? How can you overcome those obstacles?
- What additional information do you need to decide on your next steps?

5 School-Based or District-Based Options

Leaving the classroom doesn't mean you have to leave schools altogether. It means you're ready for a new challenge in the same or a different place. School-based jobs are varied and present various new challenges that may be exciting to a person who has spent a lot of time in the classroom and is ready to try something new. Since you interact with these folks regularly or at least have access to speaking with folks in these positions, I strongly recommend you talk to colleagues about what they do in their jobs, what they like about it, and what they don't like about it. These candid conversations can be constructive when trying to make a decision. Additionally, many schools support educators in-house, helping you get another certification or degree to support the district differently.

Since I was in the classroom for 16 years, I often asked for new responsibilities. I joined committees and tested the waters of other jobs whenever I could. However, despite having the opportunity to mentor new teachers or host student teachers, I never got to be the instructional coach I wanted to be in the school I was in the longest. We tried to set up a structure that would work, and ultimately, after a teacher went out on sick leave, I had to take on different roles outside of the coaching role. This was very disappointing but not at all surprising. We never committed something to writing, so I was at the mercy of what the school needed. And this one misstep gave me the push I needed to leave that job. I loved working in that school, and I did it for nearly a decade,

 DOI: 10.4324/9781003450702-6

but it was time for me to move on, and when this last attempt to stretch me fell through, I was truly ready to take the bigger leap into a new school environment.

Because of this change of circumstances, I applied for the Teacher Center position again, and this time, I finally got it. The opportunity to interview and move their process and participate in the amazing professional learning they provided also set me up for the series of moves I would make after that. Sometimes, being attached to where you work can be an inhibitor to further growth. I learned that the hard way. That being said, being forced out of my comfort zone, although not ideal, worked for me.

Remember, when you work in a school, you are still dealing with school leadership, and many of the same challenges you face in the classroom will follow you to other positions, especially if you stay in the same district. There are certainly pros and cons to moving into a new position, both in and out of the community you already know, but this can vary on every level. And honestly, sometimes you won't feel this acutely until you make a move. It's important to give yourself grace as you settle into the new role – ask many questions and take every opportunity to ensure the new role is a good fit.

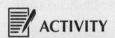 ACTIVITY

As you read through this chapter, you will see a variety of school-based or district-based positions and the qualifications needed to make these jobs possible. Again, this is a reminder that you don't need to read this chapter from beginning to end – skim through it, find the jobs you are interested in, and go from there. Keep a list of additional questions you might have, and do your research.

Guidance Counselor

Being a school guidance counselor entails a multifaceted role that focuses on supporting students' academic, social, and emotional development daily and it is likely different depending on the grade level you are working with. Typically, a school guidance counselor's daily responsibilities encompass the following:

- Student Counseling: Much of a counselor's day is spent in one-on-one or group counseling sessions with students. They provide a safe and confidential environment for students to discuss academic concerns, personal issues, and emotional challenges. These sessions involve active listening, empathy, and the development of coping strategies.
- Academic Support: Counselors work closely with students to ensure they are on track academically. They help students set academic goals, choose appropriate courses, and develop study skills. They also provide information on college and career options, assisting students in planning their educational paths.
- Crisis Intervention: In emergencies or crises affecting students, such as bullying, family issues, or mental health concerns, counselors play a critical role in providing immediate support and referrals to appropriate resources.
- College and Career Counseling: Counselors guide students through the college application process, including advising on college selection, SAT/ACT preparation, scholarship opportunities, and financial aid. They also help students explore potential career paths and post-graduation options.
- Support for Special Populations: Counselors may work with specific student populations, such as students with disabilities, English language learners, or those experiencing homelessness, to ensure they can access appropriate services and accommodations.
- Collaboration with Teachers and Parents: Counselors collaborate closely with teachers to identify and address students' needs. They also communicate regularly with

parents and guardians to provide updates on student progress and offer guidance on parenting and student support strategies.

- Classroom Presentations: Counselors often conduct classroom presentations on topics such as study skills, conflict resolution, anti-bullying initiatives, and career exploration to enhance students' personal and academic development.
- Data Analysis: Counselors analyze data related to student performance, attendance, and behavior to identify trends and areas where interventions may be needed. They use this data to inform their counseling strategies and interventions.
- Administrative Tasks: Counselors also have administrative responsibilities, including maintaining student records, scheduling counseling appointments, and coordinating standardized testing.
- Professional Development: Staying up to date with the latest trends and research in counseling and education is essential. Counselors often engage in professional development opportunities and attend workshops and conferences to enhance their skills and knowledge.
- Advocacy: Counselors advocate for the well-being and academic success of students by working with school administrators and policymakers to address issues affecting the school community. They may also advocate for individual students' needs.
- Self-Care: Given the emotional demands of the role, self-care is crucial for counselors. They need to manage their well-being to provide effective support to students.

In essence, being a school guidance counselor involves a dynamic and compassionate approach to addressing the diverse needs of students, aiming to empower them to succeed academically, socially, and emotionally while navigating the challenges of school and life. The day-to-day work of a counselor revolves around creating a nurturing and inclusive environment where students can thrive.

Social Worker

Social workers in schools play a critical role in supporting the well-being and development of students. Their primary focus is on addressing the social, emotional, and behavioral needs of students to ensure a safe and supportive school environment. Here are some of the key responsibilities and functions of school social workers:

Counseling and Mental Health Support:
- Provide individual and group counseling to students dealing with a range of social and emotional issues, such as family problems, grief, trauma, anxiety, depression, and anger management.
- Conduct assessments to identify students with mental health concerns and work with them to develop coping strategies and intervention plans.
- Offer crisis intervention and support to students facing emergencies or critical situations.

Behavioral Intervention:
- Collaborate with teachers and other school staff to address behavioral issues and develop behavior intervention plans (BIPs) for students with challenging behaviors.
- Help students develop self-regulation and social skills to improve their behavior in the classroom and social settings.

Support for At-Risk Students:
- Identify and work with students at risk of academic failure, truancy, or dropping out of school. Develop intervention plans to keep them engaged in their education.
- Assist homeless students, foster children, and other vulnerable populations in accessing essential resources and support services.

Family and Home Support:
- Work closely with families to address issues that may impact a student's well-being and academic performance. Provide resources and referrals to community services when needed.

- Conduct home visits to assess family situations and provide necessary support.

Collaboration with School Staff:
- Collaborate with teachers, administrators, and other school personnel to create a supportive and inclusive school environment. Attend team meetings to discuss students' needs and progress.

Special Education Services:
- Assist in the identification and evaluation of students with disabilities. Contribute to developing Individualized Education Programs (IEPs) and support special education students.

Prevention and Education:
- Offer prevention programs and educational workshops on topics such as bullying prevention, conflict resolution, substance abuse, and mental health awareness.
- Promote a positive school culture by fostering student respect, empathy, and tolerance.

Advocacy and Referrals:
- Advocate for students' rights and needs within the school system and the broader community.
- Connect students and families with external resources and services, including mental health agencies, social services, healthcare providers, and community organizations.

Data and Documentation:
- Maintain accurate records of student assessments, counseling sessions, and interventions.
- Collect and analyze data related to student behavior and well-being to inform decision-making and program planning.

Professional Development:
- Stay current with best practices in school social work, mental health, and education by participating in professional development and training opportunities.

Overall, school social workers play a crucial role in addressing students' social and emotional aspects, helping them overcome challenges, and fostering a positive and inclusive school environment that supports their overall growth and development. We all know this as we have worked with them in our schools. They are compassionate and knowledgeable. For me, they were lifesavers when I had students in crisis. Both roles are vital in a school community.

So, how does one become a school guidance counselor or social worker? Some specific credentials and qualifications are typically required. The exact requirements can vary depending on the state, school district, and level of education, but here are the common credentialing and educational pathways for each profession:

School Guidance Counselor	School Social Worker
Education: Typically, a master's degree in school counseling or a closely related field is required. Some states may accept a master's in counseling psychology or a related discipline, provided it includes coursework in school counseling.	Education: School social workers usually hold a master's degree in social work (MSW) from an accredited program. Some states may accept a bachelor's degree in social work with relevant experience for certain positions.
Licensure or Certification: Most states require school guidance counselors to be licensed or certified. This often involves passing a state-specific examination and meeting additional requirements, such as completing supervised counseling experience.	Licensure or Certification: Most states require school social workers to be licensed or certified as social workers. This involves passing a state-specific examination and completing supervised social work experience.

School Guidance Counselor	School Social Worker
School Counselor Certification: Some states have specific school counselor certification programs. Completing an approved program and meeting its requirements can lead to state certification.	School Social Worker Certification: Some states offer school social worker certification in addition to social work licensure. This certification may require additional coursework or training specific to school social work.
Continuing Education: School counselors are typically required to engage in continuing education to maintain their licensure or certification. This may involve taking additional courses or workshops related to counseling and education.	Continuing Education: School social workers must often participate in ongoing professional development and continuing education to maintain their licenses or certifications.
Supervised Experience: Many states require several supervised counseling hours in a school setting as part of the licensure or certification process.	Supervised Experience: Many states mandate a specific number of supervised social work hours, which may include experience in a school setting as part of the licensure or certification process.
Professional Associations: Joining professional organizations like the American School Counselor Association (ASCA) can provide guidance counselors with access to resources, networking opportunities, and professional development.	Professional Associations: Joining professional organizations like the School Social Work Association of America (SSWAA) can provide school social workers with resources, advocacy support, and networking opportunities.

It's crucial to check with the state education department and licensing board in your specific state for the most accurate and up-to-date information on the requirements for becoming a school guidance counselor or social worker. Additionally, individual school districts may have hiring preferences and require additional qualifications or certifications beyond state requirements.

While school social workers and guidance counselors play essential roles in supporting students, their areas of focus and training differ. Guidance counselors primarily concentrate on academic and career development, whereas school social workers address social, emotional, and behavioral issues, emphasizing mental health and family support. Often, schools employ both professionals to provide comprehensive support for students' overall well-being.

Leadership

There are whole books on leadership that are worthy of a read if you choose this path. I wrote *From Teacher to Leader*, about transitioning from classroom teacher to leadership. The adjustment was great despite what I thought it would be like when I was watching from my classroom. It is easy as a seasoned classroom teacher to think that you'd be better at your leader's job when things don't go the way you want them to; however, now that I have been a leader, I would say that good leaders make the job look easy and protect their teachers from a lot of nonsense that just would make the day to day even harder than it can be. Being a leader is harder than it looks, and truly exceptional leaders are as rare as some celestial phenomena.

Building-Level Leadership

In a school district, various building-level leadership positions play critical roles in overseeing the daily operations of individual schools. These positions typically work under the direction of the school principal and district administrators. Here are some common building-level leadership positions and their responsibilities:

Title	Role	Responsibilities
Principal	The principal is the chief administrator of a school and is responsible for its overall operation.	• Oversee curriculum and instructional programs. • Manage school staff, including teachers and support personnel. • Set school goals and develop improvement plans. • Ensure a safe and positive school environment. • Handle budgeting and resource allocation. • Interact with parents, students, and community members.
Assistant Principal (AP)	Assists the principal in school management and often handles specific areas of responsibility.	• Discipline and behavior management. • Student activities and extracurricular programs. • Staff evaluations and professional development. • Administrative duties as delegated by the principal.
Dean of Students or Student Affairs Coordinator	Focuses on student behavior, discipline, and student life.	• Enforce school policies and discipline procedures. • Promote a positive school culture. • Coordinate student activities and events. • Support students' social and emotional well-being.
Instructional Coach or Curriculum Specialist	Supports teachers in improving instruction and curriculum delivery.	• Provide professional development to teachers. • Assist with curriculum development and alignment. • Analyze student data to inform instructional strategies. • Observe and provide feedback to teachers.

School-Based or District-Based Options

Title	Role	Responsibilities
Special Education Coordinator or Director	Oversees special education services and programs.	• Ensure compliance with special education laws and regulations. • Develop and implement Individualized Education Plans (IEPs). • Collaborate with teachers and parents to support students with disabilities. • Manage the special education staff.
Librarian or Media Specialist	Manages the school library and support information literacy.	• Curate library resources and materials. • Teach research and digital literacy skills. • Collaborate with teachers to integrate technology and information resources into the curriculum.
Lead Teacher or Department Chair	Leads a subject-area department or grade level.	• Facilitate curriculum development and alignment. • Support teacher collaboration and professional growth. • Serve as a liaison between teachers and school administration.
School Nurse	Promotes student health and well-being.	• Provide health assessments and care for students. • Administer medications and first aid. • Develop health and safety protocols. • Educate students and staff on health-related topics.

School-Based or District-Based Options

These building-level leadership positions are crucial for maintaining the day-to-day operations of schools, fostering a positive learning environment and supporting students' academic and social growth. Each role contributes to the school's overall success and helps ensure that it meets its educational goals and objectives.

District-Office Leadership

Central or district-level leadership positions in a school district play a pivotal role in overseeing the broader educational system, shaping policies, allocating resources, and ensuring that the schools function effectively. The folks in this level of leadership require different certifications than building-level leaders and are responsible for the effectiveness of the systems that exist at large. Here are some common district-level leadership positions and job descriptions:

Title	Role	Responsibilities
Superintendent	The superintendent is the highest-ranking official in the school district and is responsible for its overall administration and educational leadership.	● Develop and implement district policies and strategic plans. ● Manage district budgets and resource allocation. ● Provide visionary leadership and direction to improve student outcomes. ● Oversee curriculum development and instructional programs. ● Communicate and collaborate with the school board, community, and stakeholders. ● Ensure compliance with state and federal education laws and regulations.

Title	Role	Responsibilities
Assistant Superintendent	Assists the superintendent in various aspects of district administration and often oversees specific areas.	● Supervise and evaluate principals and school leaders. ● Manage district operations, such as transportation or human resources. ● Implement district-wide initiatives, policies, and procedures. ● Collaborate with the superintendent on strategic planning and decision-making.
Chief Academic Officer (CAO) or Chief Instructional Officer (CIO)	Focuses on curriculum, instruction, and educational programs across the district.	● Develop and align curriculum to educational standards. ● Oversee professional development for teachers and staff. ● Analyze student performance data and assessment results. ● Monitor and improve instructional practices and student achievement. ● Implement research-based educational strategies.

School-Based or District-Based Options

Title	Role	Responsibilities
Chief Financial Officer (CFO) or Director of Finance	Manages the district's financial operations and budget.	• Develop and oversee the district's budget. • Ensure fiscal accountability and compliance. • Allocate resources to schools and programs. • Monitor financial health and sustainability.
Director of Human Resources	Oversees personnel management, including hiring, recruitment, and labor relations.	• Recruit and hire teachers and staff. • Develop and implement personnel policies and procedures. • Manage employee benefits and compensation. • Address labor relations and collective bargaining agreements.
Director of Special Education	Coordinates special education services and programs across the district.	• Ensure compliance with special education laws and regulations. • Develop and implement Individualized Education Plans (IEPs). • Oversee special education staff and support services. • Collaborate with parents and advocacy groups.

Title	Role	Responsibilities
Director of Technology Integration or Chief Technology Officer (CTO)	Manages the district's technology infrastructure and integration efforts.	● Oversee technology planning and infrastructure development. ● Facilitate the integration of technology into teaching and learning. ● Ensure data security and privacy compliance. ● Manage technology budgets and resources.
Director of Curriculum and Assessment	Focuses on curriculum development, assessment, and data analysis.	● Develop and align curriculum to educational standards. ● Implement and monitor assessment programs. ● Analyze student data to inform instructional decisions. ● Coordinate curriculum revisions and improvements.
Director of Community Relations or Public Relations	Manages district communications, public relations, and community engagement.	● Develop and implement communication strategies. ● Manage media relations and crisis communication. ● Engage with parents, community members, and stakeholders. ● Promote positive public perception of the district.

School-Based or District-Based Options

Title	Role	Responsibilities
Director of Facilities or Chief Operations Officer (COO)	Oversees the maintenance and management of district facilities.	● Ensure safe and well-maintained school buildings and grounds. ● Manage construction and renovation projects. ● Monitor compliance with safety regulations. ● Allocate and manage facility budgets.

These district-level leadership positions are essential for effective governance, decision-making, and the overall success of a school district. They collaborate to support schools, teachers, and students while adhering to district policies and educational goals. Each role has a specific focus, contributing to the district's mission of providing a quality education to all students.

Instructional Coach

A school instructional coach plays a crucial role in supporting teachers and improving teaching practices within a school or district. Not every district is lucky enough to have the funds for this role, but those that do benefit from having a person with instructional or content-level expertise who is not in administration. Because this person is not an administrator responsible for evaluation, they can often win trust and make real improvements in classroom learning so long as they aren't made to do administrative tasks since they don't typically have a class load of their own.

The day-to-day responsibilities of an instructional coach can vary depending on the specific school, grade level, subject area, and the teachers' needs. However, some everyday tasks and activities typically associated with this role are:

Teacher Collaboration:

- Collaborate with teachers and other instructional staff to identify their professional development needs and goals.
- Conduct one-on-one and group meetings with teachers to discuss instructional strategies, curriculum design, and student achievement.

Observation and Feedback:

- Observe teachers in the classroom to assess their instructional methods, classroom management, and student engagement.
- Provide constructive feedback to teachers based on observations, highlighting strengths and areas for improvement.

Professional Development:

- Plan and deliver professional development workshops, training sessions, and workshops for teachers.
- Identify and curate resources, research, and best practices to support teacher growth and development.

Data Analysis:

- Analyze student performance data, assessment results, and other relevant data to identify trends and areas for improvement.
- Collaborate with teachers to set goals and action plans based on data analysis.

Modeling Best Practices:

- Demonstrate effective teaching strategies and instructional techniques through modeling lessons or co-teaching with teachers.
- Showcase how to implement research-based practices in the classroom.

Curriculum Development:

- Assist in the development and implementation of curriculum materials and resources that align with educational standards and best practices.
- Provide guidance on curriculum mapping, lesson planning, and technology integration.

Resource Sharing:

- Share relevant instructional resources, including lesson plans, teaching materials, and educational technologies, with teachers.
- Help teachers access and navigate educational platforms and digital resources.

Teacher Reflection and Goal Setting:

- Encourage teachers to reflect on their teaching practices and set professional growth goals.
- Support teachers in creating action plans to achieve their goals.

Data-Driven Decision-Making:

- Promote a culture of data-driven decision-making among teachers and administrators.
- Collaborate with school leadership to develop strategies for improving student outcomes based on data.

Teacher Support:

- Offer emotional and professional support to teachers, especially during challenging times.
- Act as a mentor and advocate for teacher well-being and career development.

Parent and Community Engagement:

- Collaborate with parents and the community to promote a supportive learning environment.

- Facilitate parent–teacher conferences and meetings when needed.

Documentation and Reporting:

- Maintain records of teacher interactions, observations, and professional development activities.
- Report progress and outcomes to school leadership and district administrators.

Professional Learning Communities (PLCs): Facilitate or participate in PLCs where teachers collaborate and share insights, strategies, and resources.

Stay Informed: Stay up to date with educational research, trends, and best practices to provide relevant and effective support.

The day-to-day work of an instructional coach can be dynamic and may require flexibility to meet the unique needs of teachers and students. The ultimate goal is to improve teaching practices, enhance student learning outcomes, and contribute to the overall success of the school or district. Effective communication, collaboration, and a deep understanding of pedagogy are essential skills for an instructional coach to succeed.

Technology Integration Specialist

A technology integration specialist, also known as an educational technology specialist or tech integration coach, is an educational professional who focuses on integrating technology into the curriculum to enhance teaching and learning. Their primary role is to support educators in effectively using technology tools and resources to improve instruction and student outcomes. Teacher preparation programs are now working to ensure that new teachers are better equipped for the technological landscape that exists today. Organizations like ISTE and FETC work to support folks in this role in particular as the landscape is ever-changing.

Here's an overview of what a technology integration specialist does and how to become one:

Professional Development: Provide training and professional development for teachers on using technology effectively in the classroom.

Curriculum Integration: Collaborate with educators to integrate technology seamlessly into existing curriculum and lesson plans.

Resource Management: Assist in selecting and managing educational technology resources, such as software, apps, and digital content.

Tech Troubleshooting: Troubleshoot technical issues and provide support to teachers and students when they encounter problems with technology.

Innovation and Experimentation: Encourage and support innovative teaching practices that leverage technology for personalized learning and engagement.

Assessment and Data Analysis: Use data and analytics to assess the impact of technology integration on student achievement and make data-driven decisions.

Stay Informed: Keep up to date with emerging technology trends and tools in education and share this knowledge with educators.

Do these job responsibilities seem well suited for what you'd like to do next? Here are some of the steps you may have to take in order to be competitive for this job.

1   Educational Background: Obtain a bachelor's degree in education, instructional technology, or a related field. A degree in education provides a strong foundation in teaching practices, while a degree in instructional technology focuses on using technology in education.
2   Teaching Experience: Gain classroom teaching experience as an educator. To be an effective technology integration specialist, it's essential to understand the challenges and needs of teachers.

3 Master's Degree (Optional): While not always required, many technology integration specialists have a master's degree in educational technology, instructional design, or a related field. A master's degree can enhance your knowledge and career prospects.

4 Professional Development: Engage in ongoing professional development related to educational technology. Attend workshops, conferences, and courses to stay current with technology trends and best practices.

5 Certification (Optional): Some states and school districts offer certification for educational technology specialists. Earning certification can demonstrate your expertise in this field.

6 Tech Proficiency: Develop strong technical skills in various hardware and software tools commonly used in educational settings. Familiarity with learning management systems, productivity software, and educational apps is essential.

7 Communication Skills: Hone your communication and interpersonal skills. Technology integration specialists must work closely with teachers, administrators, and students, so effective communication is crucial.

8 Collaboration: Cultivate collaboration skills to collaborate with educators to achieve common goals related to technology integration.

9 Networking: Build a professional network in the educational technology community. Networking can provide opportunities for collaboration and career advancement.

10 Experience with Diverse Learning Environments: Gain experience working with students of various age groups and in different educational settings, such as K-12 schools, higher education, or corporate training.

11 Job Search: Look for job openings for technology integration specialists in schools, districts, or educational technology companies. Tailor your application to highlight your relevant experience and skills.

Technology integration specialists are crucial in helping schools and educators leverage technology to enhance teaching and learning. Their expertise and support can improve student engagement and outcomes, making this a rewarding career path for those passionate about education and technology.

Higher Education

Transitioning from a K-12 teaching career to a higher education role can be a rewarding move for educators who want to work in a college or university setting. However, this particular job search is not for the faint of heart. In my experience, despite being a published author whose books are in many pre-service education classes on assessment, I haven't even been able to break into this field yet. Regardless of this hiccup, I make it a point to speak to pre-service teachers and try to stay relevant in the conversation.

Here are steps to help K-12 teachers get involved in higher education jobs:

1 Self-Assessment: Reflect on your skills, expertise, and interests to identify the specific higher education roles that align with your goals. Consider whether you prefer teaching, research, administration, or a combination.
2 Advanced Education: Many higher education positions, especially faculty roles, require advanced degrees. Pursue a master's or doctoral degree in your field or a related area if you haven't already. A Ph.D. is often necessary for tenure-track positions.
3 Teaching Experience: Your K-12 teaching experience is valuable. Highlight your teaching accomplishments, classroom management skills, curriculum development, and instructional strategies when applying for higher education positions.

4 Research and Publications: If you're interested in academic positions, engage in research and publish scholarly articles or books in your field. Demonstrating research expertise can be crucial for faculty roles.

5 Networking: Attend academic conferences and events in your field to network with higher education professionals. Building connections can lead to job opportunities and collaborations.

6 Adjunct Teaching: Start by applying for adjunct or part-time teaching positions at local colleges or universities. Adjunct roles often require a master's degree or higher. Gain experience in higher education settings and expand your network.

7 Teaching Portfolio: Create a teaching portfolio that showcases your K-12 teaching experience, educational philosophy, sample lesson plans, and student outcomes. Highlight your ability to engage and educate students effectively.

8 Seek Mentoring: Find mentors who work in higher education and can guide the transition. They can provide insights into job opportunities, application strategies, and expectations in academia.

9 Professional Development: Continue your professional development by attending workshops, seminars, and courses related to higher education and your chosen field.

10 CV/Resume Update: Tailor your CV or resume to emphasize your academic qualifications, relevant professional experiences, and educational contributions. Include any publications, conference presentations, or workshops you've conducted. I discussed this at length earlier in Chapter 2.

11 Apply for Positions: Monitor job listings at colleges and universities for positions that match your qualifications and interests. Apply for faculty, lecturer, or administrative roles as they become available.

12 Interview Preparation: Prepare for interviews by researching the institutions, understanding their mission and culture, and practicing your responses to common higher education interview questions.

13 Demonstrate Passion: During interviews and in your application materials, convey your passion for teaching, learning, and contributing to the academic community.

14 Stay Persistent: The transition to higher education can be competitive. Be persistent and patient in your job search. It may take time to secure a position that aligns with your goals.

15 Stay Current: Stay informed about trends, developments, and challenges in higher education by reading academic journals, attending conferences, and participating in relevant online communities.

Remember that the higher education job market can be competitive, and it may take time to secure a position. Be open to different roles, such as adjunct teaching, lecturer positions, or instructional design, as stepping stones to a full-time faculty or administrative position in higher education. Networking and showcasing your passion for teaching and learning are key factors in a successful transition.

You may have heard terms like adjunct or full-time tenured professor before, but you aren't sure which would be best for you. An adjunct professor, often called an "adjunct," is a part-time or temporary faculty member at a college or university. Adjunct professors are typically hired to teach specific courses on a contractual or semester-to-semester basis, rather than holding a permanent, tenure-track position. Here are the key differences between an adjunct professor and a professor:

Adjunct Professor	Professor (Tenured or Tenure Track)
Part-Time Status: Adjunct professors are part time instructors. They are not typically considered full-time employees of the institution.	Full-Time Status: Professors, especially those with tenure or on a tenure track, are typically full-time faculty members. They hold permanent positions at the institution.
Contractual Basis: They are contracted, often for a single semester or academic year, to teach specific courses. Contracts may be renewed based on need and performance.	Long-Term Commitment: Tenure-track professors undergo a rigorous evaluation process and, if granted tenure, have job security for the long term. Non-tenure-track professors may have renewable contracts but are often on a career path leading to tenure.
Teaching Focus: Adjuncts primarily focus on teaching. While they may engage in some research or scholarly activities, their primary responsibility is delivering courses and supporting student learning.	Teaching and Research: Professors engage in a combination of teaching, research, and service. Research and scholarly activity are essential components of their responsibilities in addition to teaching.

Adjunct Professor	Professor (Tenured or Tenure Track)
Limited Job Security: Adjunct positions are generally not tenured or tenure track. As a result, adjuncts often have less job security and may not have access to the same benefits and support as full-time faculty.	Institutional Engagement: Professors are often involved in departmental and institutional governance, curriculum development, and advising students.
Varied Backgrounds: Adjuncts come from a variety of backgrounds. Some are experienced educators with advanced degrees, while others may have professional expertise in their field but limited teaching experience.	Advanced Degrees: They typically hold advanced degrees, such as a Ph.D., in their field. The highest academic rank is often "full professor."
Varied Career Goals: Many adjuncts teach part time while pursuing other careers or interests. Some may aspire to transition to full-time faculty positions, while others are content with their part-time roles.	Career Commitment: Becoming a professor is often a long-term career commitment, with the intention of advancing through the academic ranks and contributing significantly to the field.

Adjunct Professor	Professor (Tenured or Tenure Track)
Flexible Scheduling: Adjuncts may teach courses during the day, evening, or online, providing flexibility in scheduling.	Stable Position: Tenured professors have job security and the protection of academic freedom, which allows them to pursue research and scholarship without fear of dismissal for their views.

The primary distinction between an adjunct professor and a professor lies in their employment status, job security, teaching load, and career trajectory. Adjuncts are often hired on a temporary basis with a primary focus on teaching, while professors, especially those on the tenure track, have a more comprehensive role that includes teaching, research, and institutional involvement. Both roles contribute to the educational experience in higher education, but they offer different levels of stability and opportunities for career advancement.

Being a professor, full- or part time, isn't the only way to get involved with higher education. These institutions offer a wide range of administrative roles that contribute to the effective operation and management of the institution. The specific responsibilities and day-to-day activities vary depending on the position and the department or office in which the administrator works. Here are some common administrative roles in higher education and an overview of what the day-to-day work may entail:

Title	Role	Day-to-Day Responsibilities
Registrar	The registrar manages student records, academic calendars, course scheduling, and registration processes.	• Maintain and update student records. • Coordinate course registration and enrollment. • Manage academic calendars and scheduling. • Ensure compliance with academic policies and regulations.
Admissions Director	Admissions directors oversee the recruitment and admission of students to the institution.	• Develop and implement recruitment strategies. • Review and evaluate applications. • Coordinate admission events and interviews. • Collaborate with academic departments to assess admission criteria.
Financial Aid Director	Financial aid directors manage financial aid programs and assist students with funding options.	• Administer financial aid applications and awards. • Advise students on financial aid options. • Ensure compliance with federal and state financial aid regulations. • Monitor and manage financial aid budgets.
Student Affairs Director	Student affairs directors oversee student services, campus life, and extracurricular activities.	• Coordinate student orientation programs. • Manage residence life and housing services. • Support student clubs and organizations. • Address student concerns and conduct disciplinary procedures.

Title	Role	Day-to-Day Responsibilities
Academic Dean	Academic deans lead academic departments or schools within the institution.	• Oversee curriculum development and assessment. • Manage faculty and staff within the department. • Collaborate with other deans and administrators. • Address academic issues and support student success.
Director of Institutional Research	Institutional research directors collect and analyze data to inform decision-making.	• Collect and analyze institutional data. • Prepare reports for administrators and external stakeholders. • Research enrollment trends and student outcomes. • Support accreditation processes.
Chief Diversity Officer	Chief diversity officers promote diversity, equity, and inclusion on campus.	• Develop and implement diversity initiatives and programs. • Collaborate with campus groups and committees. • Address diversity-related issues and concerns. • Promote a welcoming and inclusive campus environment.

School-Based or District-Based Options

Title	Role	Day-to-Day Responsibilities
Development Officer (Fundraising)	Development officers lead fundraising efforts and donor relations.	• Identify and cultivate potential donors. • Plan and execute fundraising campaigns. • Build relationships with alumni and philanthropic organizations. • Manage donor databases and gift processing.
Director of Career Services	Career services directors assist students with career exploration and job placement.	• Provide career counseling and advising. • Organize job fairs and networking events. • Develop and maintain employer partnerships. • Support students in resume writing and interview preparation.
Facilities Manager	Facilities managers oversee campus facilities, maintenance, and construction projects.	• Manage maintenance and custodial staff. • Coordinate building maintenance and repairs. • Plan and oversee construction and renovation projects. • Ensure campus safety and compliance with regulations.

These are just a few examples of administrative roles in higher education. Day-to-day responsibilities can vary widely depending on the specific position, the size and type of institution, and the current priorities and projects within the department or office. Administrative roles often require strong communication, leadership, organizational, and problem-solving skills to effectively manage higher education institutions' needs and challenges.

Research

You love to research, and while you are working on your next degree, you decide that you want to keep doing the research instead of going back to a traditional education job. Research jobs are essential for moving education and specific fields of study forward. Working in higher education where you spend time doing the quantitative or qualitative research may be what you need to get reinvigorated. Of course, higher education isn't the only place to do research. You can get involved with private research firms and companies where you can stay close to the content you initially fell in love with.

Getting involved in research work as an alternative career pathway for educators can be a rewarding and intellectually stimulating transition. It allows educators to leverage their classroom experience and contribute to the broader field of education. Here are steps educators can take to embark on a research-oriented career:

1   Identify Your Research Interests: Start by identifying your specific research interests within the field of education. Consider what aspects of education, teaching, or learning fascinate you the most. Your passion will drive your research endeavors.
2   Build a Strong Educational Foundation: Ensure that you have a solid educational background in your chosen field. While some educators may have a bachelor's degree in education, pursuing a master's or doctoral degree in a

specialized area can provide the necessary research skills and expertise.

3 Engage in Professional Development: Attend workshops, courses, and conferences related to research methods, data analysis, and educational research. These opportunities will enhance your research skills and knowledge.

4 Collaborate with Researchers: Seek collaboration opportunities with established researchers or research teams. Collaborative projects can help you gain research experience and access valuable resources.

5 Conduct Action Research: Start by conducting action research within your own classroom. Action research involves systematically studying and improving your teaching practices. This can serve as a valuable entry point into educational research.

6 Publish and Present Findings: Share your research findings by publishing articles in education journals or presenting at conferences. This will help establish your credibility as a researcher and expand your network within the research community.

7 Join Research Networks: Become a member of educational research networks or organizations. These groups often provide resources, support, and opportunities for collaboration.

8 Explore Alternative Roles: Consider roles in educational research institutions, think tanks, policy organizations, or educational technology companies. These organizations often hire educators with research expertise to conduct studies and contribute to educational innovation.

9 Seek Funding Opportunities: Look for research grants, fellowships, and scholarships to support your research projects financially. Many organizations and foundations offer funding for educational research.

10 Become a Research Consultant: Offer your expertise as a research consultant to educational institutions or organizations requiring project research assistance. This can be a flexible and independent way to engage in research.

11 Stay Informed: Stay updated on the latest trends, research methodologies, and developments in the field of

education. Reading research publications and participating in relevant webinars and forums is crucial.

12 Network and Collaborate: Build a strong network of fellow researchers, educators, and professionals in the field. Collaborate on research projects and seek mentorship from experienced researchers.

13 Contribute to Policy Discussions: Use your research findings to support policy discussions and educational reforms. Your insights as an educator-researcher can inform decision-making in education.

14 Balance Teaching and Research: If you choose to continue teaching while engaging in research, find a balance that works for you. Some educators choose to teach part time or take on research-related roles within educational institutions.

15 Be Patient and Persistent: Transitioning into a research-oriented career may take time. Be patient, persist, and refine your research skills and expertise.

Remember that education research is a diverse field, encompassing a wide range of topics and methodologies. Educators who embark on this alternative career pathway have the opportunity to make meaningful contributions to improving education and advancing knowledge in the field.

 ACTIVITY

Regardless of the field or discipline, research careers require specific skills and attributes to conduct high-quality research, analyze data, and communicate findings effectively. Here are some essential skills for research careers that you will likely have already developed as an educator. As you read this list, highlight areas you are strong in and jot down job experience that supports your assertion.

Research Methodology: Understanding various research methods, including qualitative and quantitative approaches, surveys, experiments, case studies, and observational techniques, is fundamental. Researchers must choose the most appropriate methods for their research questions.

Critical Thinking: Researchers must possess strong critical thinking skills to evaluate existing literature, formulate research questions, and analyze data objectively. Critical thinking involves questioning assumptions and examining evidence critically.

Problem-solving: Identifying research problems, designing studies to address them, and proposing solutions is crucial. Researchers should be adept at breaking down complex issues into manageable research questions.

Data Collection: Depending on the research design, researchers should know how to collect data effectively, whether through surveys, interviews, observations, experiments, or document analysis. They should also ensure data reliability and validity.

Data Analysis: Proficiency in data analysis tools and software, such as statistical packages (e.g., SPSS, R, or Python), is essential for quantitative researchers. Qualitative researchers should be skilled in coding and thematic analysis.

Literature Review: Conducting a thorough literature review is a foundational research skill. Researchers should be able to identify existing studies, synthesize findings, and situate their research within the broader academic context.

Attention to Detail: Researchers must be meticulous in data collection, organization, and analysis to avoid errors or bias in their research findings.

Ethical Research: Adhering to ethical guidelines and obtaining informed consent when working with human subjects is paramount. Researchers must understand ethical considerations and conduct research with integrity.

Writing and Communication: Effective written and oral communication skills are vital for presenting research findings to peers, publishing journal articles, and conveying complex ideas to a broader audience. Researchers should be able to write concisely and persuasively.

Time Management: Research often involves managing multiple tasks simultaneously, including data collection, analysis, and writing. Researchers must prioritize and meet deadlines efficiently.

Adaptability: Research projects can evolve, and unexpected challenges may arise. Researchers should be adaptable and open to modifying research designs or methodologies.

Quantitative and Qualitative Skills: Depending on the research approach, researchers may need skills specific to quantitative or qualitative research, such as statistical analysis or coding.

Project Management: Large-scale research projects may require project management skills to keep the research on track, allocate resources effectively, and ensure timely completion.

Computer Skills: Proficiency in using research software, data analysis tools, and reference management software is crucial for efficient research.

Collaboration: Many research projects involve collaboration with other researchers, and teamwork skills are essential for successful group research endeavors.

Presentation Skills: Researchers should be able to present their findings in a clear, organized, and engaging manner at conferences, seminars, or meetings.

Interdisciplinary Knowledge: Depending on the research area, interdisciplinary knowledge can be valuable for connecting research findings to broader contexts and applications. This is one area that I'm excited about. I work with educators in the humanities, mostly to help them cross disciplines to enhance the learning experience for students.

These skills are transferable across various research careers and disciplines. Researchers may specialize in one or more of these areas based on their specific roles and research interests. Continuous professional development and staying current with advancements in research methods and technology are also essential for success in research careers.

Educators who want to get into research can work in various settings and institutions that focus on educational research and development. Some places where educators can find research opportunities are:

- Universities and Colleges: Many higher education institutions have research centers, departments, or institutes dedicated to educational research. These settings often offer researchers, postdoctoral fellows, and research assistants positions.
- Educational Research Organizations: Numerous research organizations specialize in educational research and policy analysis. Examples include the American Educational Research Association (AERA) and the National Center for Education Research (NCER).
- K-12 School Districts: Some school districts hire educators with research expertise to conduct internal research and evaluation studies. These roles may involve assessing the effectiveness of educational programs and interventions.
- Educational Technology Companies: EdTech companies often employ educators to conduct research on the efficacy of their products and services. Research positions may involve evaluating the impact of technology on teaching and learning.
- Non-profit Organizations: Non-profits focused on education, such as the Bill & Melinda Gates Foundation or the Education Trust, frequently hire researchers to study educational issues and develop evidence-based solutions.
- Think Tanks: Think tanks, including those specializing in education policy, employ researchers to conduct studies and provide insights to inform education policy decisions.
- Government Agencies: Educational research positions are available in government agencies like the U.S. Department of Education, where researchers work on policy analysis, program evaluation, and data analysis.
- Educational Assessment Organizations: Companies that develop standardized tests and assessments may hire educators with research expertise to ensure the validity and reliability of assessments.

- Educational Publishers: Educational publishers often employ researchers to develop and validate educational materials, including textbooks and online resources.
- Foundations: Many philanthropic foundations have education-related initiatives and hire researchers to assess the impact of their grants and programs.
- Research Consulting Firms: Research consulting firms specializing in education may offer opportunities for educators to work on various research projects for clients in the public and private sectors.
- Professional Associations: Educational associations and organizations, such as teacher associations or subject-specific organizations, sometimes conduct research and hire educators to lead research initiatives.
- International Organizations: Educators interested in global education research can explore opportunities with international organizations like UNESCO, the World Bank, or NGOs working on education worldwide.
- Online Learning Platforms: Online learning platforms and Massive Open Online Course (MOOC) providers hire researchers to evaluate the effectiveness of their courses and learning interventions.
- Research Fellowships: Consider applying for research fellowships or grants that allow you to pursue independent research or collaborate with established researchers in various educational contexts.

When exploring these opportunities, aligning your research interests and expertise with the organization's goals and mission is essential. Networking, attending conferences, and staying informed about job openings in the field can help educators find the right research position that suits their career goals and aspirations.

Content area specialists with in-depth expertise in a specific subject or field can pursue various research careers that align with their knowledge and passion. These careers often involve conducting research, publishing findings, and contributing to advancements in their respective disciplines. Here are some research career options for content area specialists:

Job Title	Description
Academic Researcher/ Professor	Content area specialists can pursue careers as academic researchers or professors at universities and colleges. They conduct research in their field of expertise, publish research papers, and may teach courses related to their subject area.
Research Scientist	In academic institutions or research organizations, specialists can work as research scientists, focusing on advancing knowledge in their content area. They may conduct experiments, gather data, and publish their findings.
Curriculum Developer	Specialists can work as curriculum developers, designing educational materials, textbooks, and instructional resources that align with the content area's curriculum standards. Research is often part of the process to ensure effective curriculum development.
Educational Assessment Specialist	Specialists can become experts in educational assessment, working to design and validate assessments that measure students' knowledge and skills in their content area.
Policy Analyst/ Researcher	Content area specialists can work in research and policy analysis roles, examining educational policies and their impact on the curriculum and instruction in their subject area.

Job Title	Description
Educational Consultant	Consultants with content expertise can provide guidance to schools, districts, or educational organizations on improving curriculum, instruction, and student outcomes. Research and data analysis may be a part of their consultancy work.
Subject Matter Expert (SME)	Specialists can serve as SMEs in various organizations, including educational technology companies and publishers, helping to develop educational materials and resources that align with the content area's standards and goals.
Grant Writer/ Research Development Specialist	Content area specialists can work as grant writers or research development specialists, helping educational institutions and organizations secure funding for research projects related to their subject area.
Content Area Researcher in Think Tanks	Some think tanks and research organizations hire specialists to conduct research on topics related to their field and contribute to policy discussions and reports.
Research Fellowships	Pursuing research fellowships or grants from foundations, government agencies, or educational organizations can allow specialists to conduct independent research in their areas of expertise.

Job Title	Description
Online Course Designer/ Instructional Designer	Specialists can work as online course designers or instructional designers, creating engaging and effective online courses or learning materials in their content area. Research on practical instructional design principles is often involved.
Professional Development Specialist	Specialists can become professional development trainers, providing workshops and training sessions for educators looking to improve their knowledge and teaching practices in the content area.
Research Analyst in Educational Technology	With the increasing use of technology in education, specialists can work as research analysts in educational technology companies, researching the impact of technology on learning in their content area.
Content Writer/ Author	Specialists can become content writers or authors, creating educational content, articles, books, and digital resources that share their expertise and research findings.
Museum or Cultural Institution Researcher	If their expertise is in a specific area like history, art, or science, specialists can work as researchers in museums or cultural institutions, researching exhibits and educational programs.

Content area specialists should explore opportunities that align with their passions, expertise, and career goals. Research careers for content area specialists often require strong analytical skills, research methodology knowledge, and the ability to communicate findings effectively through writing and presentations.

 **Final Thoughts**

Whether you're interested in school-based or district-based positions, higher education, or research, there are so many opportunities that you can invest your time and expertise in that offer a different kind of work and working environment. As you read through this chapter in particular, I imagine you thought about the folks you know in your district who fill these roles, and perhaps you wondered how they got into those roles or if they like them. If one of the job descriptions spoke to you, I encourage you to talk informally with the folks you know in those positions. Ask to speak with them off the record, and if you don't know someone in the position and would like to speak with someone, go on social media and ask; you'll find that most folks are incredibly generous with their time. That's how I had the opportunity to develop the playlist.

 REFLECTION QUESTIONS

- Which jobs did you read about that sound like a good fit for your interests and qualifications?
- How will a different school-based job solve the problem causing you to seek a new path?
- Who might you talk to about the position you're interested in?
- What questions would you like to ask to learn more about this position?

6 | Do I Want to Consult?

Becoming an education consultant can offer a range of benefits for individuals with a passion for education, a strong background in instruction and/or leadership, and a desire to make a positive impact on schools, educators, and students. This has been my experience for sure. But just because you have a specific skill set doesn't mean that you will like consulting. Many aspects of this job are very uncomfortable, mainly if you are accustomed to the extreme security of a tenure-based position in the school district.

For me, it just kind of happened. After I wrote my first few books, people started reaching out to me. I was still in the classroom and over the moon that people were reading my books. Already I was involved in national and state organizations, and I had the opportunity to present in my area of expertise, but I didn't have much availability. When you are in the classroom, your school-based job comes first, and what I learned very quickly is that it is a conflict of interest to make money outside of your school-based job on school time, even if you are taking days off.

Being naive initially, I skated around the rules until it became a problem in school. I was invited to speak at an assessment conference. Flattered. Excited and beyond thrilled to be mentioned among the folks whom I consider my assessment idols, I went to my principal to ask for the time off to go, but matters quickly escalated. Although I could attend conferences and present for free, being paid to speak at a conference through a stipend and expenses went against NYC's policy.

DOI: 10.4324/9781003450702-7   155

Quickly, my principal brought the matter to legal, where it was unceremoniously shut down. Eventually, I was able to strike a balance, but by the time we got there, the company running the conference was spooked and didn't want to get in trouble for bringing me. The opportunity was lost, and I was left with a free video and book because they felt so bad that I couldn't participate.

Some benefits of being an education consultant include:

- Professional Autonomy: As an education consultant, you can choose the projects you work on, the clients you collaborate with, and the areas of education you specialize in. This autonomy allows you to align your work with your passions and expertise.
- Variety of Work: Education consultants often engage in a diverse range of projects, from curriculum design and teacher training to educational technology integration and policy analysis. This variety keeps the work engaging and intellectually stimulating.
- Flexibility: Education consulting can offer a flexible schedule, allowing you to balance work with personal commitments. This flexibility can be particularly appealing to those seeking a better work–life balance.
- Impact and Contribution: Education consultants play a direct role in improving educational practices, policies, and outcomes. Your insights and recommendations can positively influence classrooms, schools, and even entire districts.
- Continuous Learning: Staying relevant as an education consultant requires ongoing learning and staying up to date with the latest trends, research, and educational best practices. This commitment to learning can be intellectually rewarding.
- Networking Opportunities: Working with various schools, educators, organizations, and policymakers allows you to build a wide network of professionals in the education field. Networking can lead to collaboration, partnerships, and new opportunities. You just never know when the

Do I Want to Consult?

relationships you develop will turn into friendships or future work.

- Creativity and Innovation: Education consultants are often free to propose innovative solutions and approaches to educational challenges. This creativity can be fulfilling for individuals who enjoy thinking outside the box.
- Financial Potential: Education consulting can be financially rewarding depending on your expertise and the demand for your services. Experienced consultants with specialized knowledge are often able to command higher fees.
- Positive Change: Consultants can drive positive change in education systems. Your recommendations can improve teaching methods, enhance student outcomes, and lead to better learning environments.
- Professional Growth: As an education consultant, you can continually expand your skill set, broaden your knowledge, and refine your expertise. This growth can lead to personal satisfaction and a strong sense of accomplishment.
- Contribution to Education System: By sharing your insights, knowledge, and experience, you contribute to the development and improvement of the broader education system. Your work can have lasting effects on education policies and practices.
- Personal Fulfillment: For those who are passionate about education and making a difference, being an education consultant can be deeply fulfilling. Seeing the positive impact of your work on students, teachers, and schools can be incredibly rewarding.
- Staying Below the Fray: When you work as a consultant, you never have to be involved in sticky district or school building politics. You will definitely hear about them and navigating that can be challenging at times, but it is nice to not be directly affected by the day-to-day BS that happens in schools at times. You can be an objective voice and that is very helpful to the folks you work with. You will also grow a global perspective, which is helpful in these matters as well.

While there are many benefits to being an education consultant, it's important to note that the role also comes with challenges, such as the need to constantly market yourself, deal with variable income, and manage the demands of multiple clients and projects. However, for individuals dedicated to improving education and with the skills to offer valuable insights, education consulting can be a rewarding and fulfilling career choice.

Established Company or Start a New One?

When I started out, I'm not sure I would have even considered myself a "real" consultant. It was largely local gigs I was getting, and the rest were just speaking engagements or informal conversations. It wasn't until 2019 that I was introduced to a reputable consulting company whose mission and body of work aligned with my own. Being so green still, I didn't know where to start and felt overwhelmed by all of the options. Plus, I was extremely nervous about leaving my stable leadership position for the unknown. It was helpful to talk to people in this company and get a real perspective of their transition into the work. It offered a legitimate perspective to ease my mind about leaping. Fortunately, this company didn't expect me to be exclusive with them, and they encouraged me to consult on my own work and theirs. Being involved with an established company made it all easier. It wasn't so lonely or scary.

There are certainly pros and cons to working for someone else. For example, since they are doing the negotiating for you, you don't set your own price, and they take a cut of what you are making. Some places may offer a flat rate for your time, including your expenses, while others pay your expenses separately. Either way, you will need to start accounting for your money yourself, as your tax situation just went from a W4 to a W9, and as an independent contractor you can write a lot of stuff off. I recommend you talk to an accountant before you get started. This was a big blind spot, and it took me a while to figure it out.

Another pro is that these established companies have accounts they already work with, and you get to work on a team sometimes. Being a consultant can be lonely, so having a team of folks doing the same work and people to report back to can create structure and more work. But someone else will take care of your insurance, paperwork, and pay, which is helpful. Make sure, though, that if you work for another company, you are clear of the boundaries so you don't create a conflict of interest for yourself. For example, if you work for a company and the school you are in wants to work with you directly, this is impossible. Because you are contractually obligated to go through the company you got the connection through, taking on that client without first speaking to the company would be ethically wrong.

When I set up my own LLC because one of my personal accounts asked me to, many expenses were associated with the company's establishment. Deciding what kind of company is also something you will want to do some research on. Here is some info to help you get started. This is not a comprehensive understanding of what these kinds of companies are. You should research and ask for advice if you go down this road.

Kind of Company	Pros	Cons
Sole Proprietorship	• Simple and low cost to set up and operate. • Complete control over the business. • Direct reporting of business income and expenses on personal tax returns (pass-through taxation). • Minimal regulatory requirements.	• Personal liability for business debts and legal issues; limited asset protection. • Limited ability to raise capital or attract investors. • Potential difficulty in transitioning or selling the business.

Kind of Company	Pros	Cons
Limited Liability Company (LLC)	• Limited personal liability, protecting personal assets from business debts and lawsuits. • Flexible management structure. • Pass-through taxation, avoiding double taxation. • Easier compliance with formalities compared to a corporation.	• Depending on the state, ongoing administrative and filing requirements may exist. • Less rigid management structure may lead to potential conflicts among members. • Limited ability to attract investors compared to a corporation.
C Corporation	• Limited personal liability; shareholders are generally not personally liable for business debts. • Ability to raise capital by issuing stock. • Potential for significant tax benefits, including deductible business expenses.	• Double taxation: Corporate profits are taxed at the corporate level, and dividends are taxed when distributed to shareholders. • More complex and costly to set up and maintain than other structures. • Greater regulatory and reporting requirements, including annual reports and shareholder meetings.

Kind of Company	Pros	Cons
S Corporation	• Limited personal liability, like a C corporation. • Pass-through taxation, avoiding double taxation. • Allows for self-employment tax savings on distributions (subject to certain IRS rules).	• Strict eligibility requirements, including restrictions on the number and type of shareholders. • Complex administrative and compliance requirements. • Limited ability to retain earnings for growth due to pass-through taxation.
Partnership	• Pass-through taxation, with profits and losses reported on partners' individual tax returns. • Shared decision-making and management among partners. • Potential for greater access to capital and resources with multiple partners.	• Personal liability for business debts and legal issues, including those incurred by other partners. • Potential for conflicts among partners regarding decision-making and profit sharing. • Need for a partnership agreement to define roles, responsibilities, and profit distribution.

Kind of Company	Pros	Cons
Limited Liability Partnership (LLP)	• Limited personal liability for partners, protecting personal assets. • Pass-through taxation. • Allows professionals in certain fields to form partnerships while limiting liability.	• Complex regulatory requirements in some states. • Potential personal liability for the negligent acts of other partners (depends on state laws).

The choice of legal structure should align with your specific business goals, risk tolerance, and tax considerations. It's advisable to consult with legal and financial professionals to make an informed decision, as the legal and tax implications can vary based on your location and industry. Additionally, your business needs may evolve, so it's essential to periodically reassess your legal structure to ensure it continues to meet your objectives. You can learn more about selecting a business structure at www.sba.gov/business-guide/launch-your-business/choose-business-structure.

How Much Should I Charge? ... It Depends

Money is always a challenging topic to talk about. Teachers often ask me how much I charge and how I determine this is the best price. It's touchy. Trying to figure out how much you are worth as a consultant and how much schools are willing to pay can be tricky. At first, I tried different numbers and waited to see if clients would pay what I asked. Often, I'd slyly ask friends I respect, "How much do you make, and how do you know it is competitive?"

Do I Want to Consult?

I knew how much we paid for some more established folks in my school and was always impressed by how glamorous it sounded. It is also evident that, as a general rule, men feel more comfortable demanding more for their time and expertise. Asking schools to pay me what I'm worth always feels a bit like a crap shoot, and I tend to devalue myself because I don't want to price myself out of what schools can afford. The work is so important to me, and I'd rather have the opportunity to be embedded in schools to make positive change. Also, I can be more flexible with my price once I know how many days they are going to commit to having me in their school and I can also be flexible if they are willing to do some of the work virtually.

Unfortunately, there is no simple answer to this question. It really depends. You need to know your market. Do some research locally on how much schools pay for different kinds of outside help. Know how much you can demand for your expertise. If you do get published, this will help you demand more as leaders will see you as an authority if you do. Make sure to choose a price that will help you cover expenses but will also make you affordable for schools.

Speaking Engagements as Opportunities to Market Yourself

After you establish that you want to be a consultant, you need to find clients. One of the best ways to do that is to present at local, national, or international conferences. There are so many opportunities to share expertise and be seen. Getting accepted to share ideas at major conferences puts you in front of many decision-makers who will ultimately be reaching out to learn more with you.

I would recommend setting reminders about when different conferences send out calls for submission to speak. At first, you will undoubtedly be speaking for free and maybe even paying to attend the conference. Not every organization allows speakers to attend for free; there may just be a discount and it is highly likely you will be responsible for your travel. This can be very costly if you are going to a conference that is far away. You will do a cost–benefit analysis in order to determine if the potential gain from the conference can offset the cost of attending. For example, recently I have been looking to expand into an international market, so I learned about an organization called The International Academic Forum (IAFOR) and I have already presented at two of their conferences, one in Paris, France, and the other in Barcelona, Spain. It still remains to be seen if either of those risks will pay off in paid gigs, but I'm hopeful about some work I could do with a team of Norwegian professors who attended my session. Additionally, being in an international format (which is so different than the education conferences in the U.S.), I was inspired to see how similar ideas I work with are being approached from around the world. It gave me hope.

Once you are on the speaking circuit for a while, you may be asked to give a keynote or a featured presentation, which usually does pay a stipend. The stipends are usually nominal unless you are a big name. Should you write a book, that will help you become a more recognizable name as it did for me. Plus once you are a published author, people in the education world will see you differently; perhaps not in your own backyard, but definitely in other locations. It was always ironic to me that my expertise was hardly known about in my own neighborhood, but across the country, they couldn't wait for me to come to their schools.

There are hybrid opportunities too where some organizations will offset the cost of travel or the conference itself if you decide to come speak. Make sure to attend sessions, bring business cards, and share on social media. Don't make it all about you and what you have to offer, but be open as a learner and interact with people. Listen to their questions and start thinking about what you do and how it might solve the problems folks are having right now.

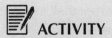 **ACTIVITY**

Do a Google search for education conferences. Find at least two local conferences or Edcamps that are free that you could drive to. Find at least two driveable conferences that would be worth paying for. Find at least two national conferences that would offer good positioning for you to market yourself and learn more about the path you want to take. Once you have your list, calendar the dates for submissions and the actual conference so that you can save where you need to. I strongly recommend making a strategy before you go if you get accepted to speak.

Drawbacks to Consulting

While education consulting offers numerous benefits, it also comes with certain drawbacks that individuals considering this career path should be aware of. Some of the drawbacks of education consulting include:

- Inconsistent Income: Education consultants often work on a project-to-project basis, leading to inconsistent income. Establishing a steady stream of clients and projects might take time, and there may be periods of financial uncertainty.
- Client Acquisition: Finding and attracting clients can be challenging, especially when starting out. Building a client base requires marketing efforts, networking, and the ability to showcase your expertise effectively.
- Competitive Market: The education consulting field can be competitive, especially in popular areas such as curriculum development, teacher training, and educational technology. Standing out among other consultants can be demanding.

- Administrative Tasks: As an independent consultant, you are responsible for managing administrative tasks such as billing, contracts, scheduling, and record-keeping. These tasks can be time-consuming and take away from your core consulting work.
- Variable Workload: The workload as an education consultant can be uneven. You might experience periods of intense work followed by slower periods, making it necessary to manage your time and finances effectively.
- Limited Benefits: Unlike traditional teaching positions, education consultants often do not receive benefits such as health insurance, retirement plans, or paid leave. You are responsible for arranging your own benefits.
- Isolation: Education consultants often work independently or remotely, which can lead to feelings of isolation. The lack of regular interactions with colleagues and peers might be challenging for those who thrive in collaborative environments.
- High Expectations: Clients may have high expectations for results, and meeting those expectations while balancing multiple projects can be stressful. It's important to manage client expectations and maintain a realistic workload.
- Travel Demands: Depending on the nature of your projects and clients, you might need to travel frequently. This can disrupt your work–life balance and add additional expenses.
- Adapting to Change: The education field is constantly evolving with new research, technologies, and practices. As a consultant, you need to stay updated and adapt quickly to changes to provide relevant and effective guidance.
- Unpredictable Projects: Clients' needs and project scopes can vary widely. You might encounter projects that are challenging, require extensive research, or involve navigating complex organizational dynamics.
- Skill Diversification: Education consultants often need to be skilled in multiple areas, including client management, marketing, project management, and research. This diversification can be demanding and requires ongoing learning.

- Dependency on Market Conditions: The demand for education consulting services can be influenced by economic conditions, changes in education policies, and shifts in educational priorities.
- Balancing Expertise and Business: Being an education consultant involves not only expertise in your chosen area but also running a business. Balancing the two aspects can be challenging, especially for those who are primarily focused on education.

It's important to carefully weigh these drawbacks against the benefits when considering a career in education consulting. While the challenges can be significant, many consultants find the rewards, personal satisfaction, and potential for positive impact on education systems to be well worth the effort.

✅ Final Thoughts

Being a consultant isn't for everyone. As a matter of fact, when I was a single mom of a young child, being a consultant would have been too much of a risk with not enough reward and I wasn't readily available to travel. Being away from home, even now as much as I am, does take a toll. There is a very specific personality who loves to be nomadic and doesn't mind being away from home more often than they aren't. Since COVID-19, it has become more prevalent to be able to do different kinds of consulting digitally if travel isn't an option, but that will greatly limit who are you able to work with. Some practical things to consider if you go down this road is which airline you are going to try to get status with, if they have a club that you can join, and which hotel and rental car chain you want to use. There are rewards to be had once you establish status and I try to use my miles at the end of each year for a family trip that I wouldn't have otherwise taken. Last year we spent our anniversary in Scotland using the miles I accumulated from the year before. This doesn't make up for my absence, but it does lessen the blow a little.

REFLECTION QUESTIONS

- Who can you talk to about being a consultant? (If you don't know anyone personally, reach out to me, I'd be happy to talk – just email me mssackstein@gmail. com and mention the book.)
- What questions or concerns do you have about being a consultant?
- What area do you see yourself as an expert in? How do you know?
- What do you have to offer that is unique that others don't have?
- What research have you done about what this work might look like for you? What do you still need to research?
- What is your conference strategy? Where do you like to present?

Do I Want to Consult?

7 EdTech

You love technology. Whenever a new tool comes out, you learn about it on social media and immediately get involved in the beta opportunities to be an early adopter. You understand the changing landscape outside of education now and you are eager to give your students the opportunity to acquire the skills needed to be successful in a world of a future that is largely not defined yet. In the midst of your experimenting, you may have been asked to be an ambassador or advisor for a particular product and so the beginning of your relationship with an EdTech company is born.

Even if the above story isn't yours, you may find a home at a new EdTech company. Being in private industry offers different experiences than a school, but your expertise and experience will be appreciated and needed for them to be successful. So how do you know which one to get involved with and in what capacity?

Types of EdTech

Educational technology (EdTech) companies encompass a wide range of organizations that leverage technology to enhance teaching and learning. These companies develop and provide various products and services designed to improve educational outcomes and streamline educational processes. Here are different types of EdTech companies:

- eLearning Platforms: These companies create online learning platforms and learning management systems (LMS) that facilitate the delivery of educational content, courses, and assessments. Examples include Canvas, Moodle, and Blackboard.
- EdTech Startups: Many startups develop innovative solutions to address specific educational challenges. They may focus on adaptive learning, gamification, language learning, or other specialized areas.
- Educational Content Providers: These companies produce digital educational content, including textbooks, e-books, videos, interactive simulations, and online lessons. Examples include Khan Academy, Coursera, and edX.
- Online Tutoring and Homework Help: Companies in this category offer online tutoring services and homework help platforms. They connect students with qualified tutors for one-on-one instruction. Examples include Chegg and Wyzant.
- Educational Games and Gamification: These companies create educational games and gamified learning platforms to engage students and make learning more interactive and enjoyable. Examples include Kahoot! and BrainPOP.
- Assessment and Analytics Tools: EdTech companies specializing in assessment and analytics provide tools for educators to assess student performance, track progress, and analyze data to inform instruction. Examples include Edmentum and NWEA.
- Coding and Computer Science Education: With the growing importance of coding and computer science skills, companies in this category offer coding boot camps, online courses, and tools for teaching coding to students of all ages. Examples include Codecademy and Tynker.
- Virtual Reality (VR) and Augmented Reality (AR) in Education: These companies leverage VR and AR technologies to create immersive educational experiences, allowing

students to explore concepts in a three-dimensional environment. Examples include Oculus Education and zSpace.

- Language Learning Platforms: EdTech companies specializing in language learning offer apps and platforms for learning foreign languages or improving language skills. Examples include Duolingo and Rosetta Stone.
- Teacher Professional Development: Companies in this category provide online courses, workshops, and resources to support teacher professional development and continuing education. Examples include Edutopia and TeachThought.
- Adaptive Learning: Adaptive learning platforms use artificial intelligence and personalized learning algorithms to tailor educational content and instruction to each student's needs and pace. Examples include DreamBox and Knewton.
- Early Childhood Education Technology: These companies focus on technology solutions for preschools and early education settings, offering interactive educational games, assessments, and classroom management tools. Examples include ABCmouse and ClassDojo.
- Student Data Privacy and Security: With increasing concerns about data privacy, companies in this category offer solutions to protect student data and ensure compliance with privacy regulations. Some examples of companies that specifically work with this are: iKeepSafe, ISTE, and Truyo. This is an area though that has a lot of laws and rules and as EdTech grows, it becomes more important for us to protect our students.
- Special Education Technology: EdTech companies specializing in special education develop tools and resources to support students with disabilities and provide educators with specialized learning materials. Examples include Tobii Dynavox and Boardmaker.
- Higher Education and EdTech for Colleges/Universities: These companies serve higher education institutions with technology solutions for admissions, enrollment management, student engagement, and online course delivery. Examples include Ellucian and Instructure (Canvas).
- Education Hardware: Companies that produce educational hardware, such as interactive whiteboards, tablets,

and educational robotics kits, play a crucial role in the integration of technology in classrooms.

These categories represent a broad spectrum of EdTech companies, and the EdTech landscape continues to evolve as technology advances and educational needs change. Many EdTech companies operate within multiple categories or develop innovative solutions that bridge different areas of education.

Positions in Technology Companies Adjacent to Education

EdTech companies often require a diverse workforce that includes individuals with both education expertise and technology skills. Positions in EdTech that are "education adjacent" typically involve roles where professionals with a strong background in education collaborate closely with technology experts to develop, implement, or support EdTech solutions. Here are some education-adjacent positions in EdTech:

- Instructional Designer: Instructional designers work closely with educators and content developers to create effective online courses, digital learning materials, and educational resources. They ensure that content aligns with educational goals and pedagogical principles while leveraging technology for optimal delivery.
- eLearning Developer: eLearning developers use their expertise in both education and technology to design and build interactive online learning modules, simulations, and multimedia educational content. They work closely with instructional designers to bring educational concepts to life in a digital format.
- Learning Experience Designer: Learning experience designers focus on enhancing the overall learning experience for students using technology. They collaborate with educators to create engaging, user-friendly digital learning environments, such as learning management systems (LMS) or virtual classrooms.

- Educational Content Specialist: Educational content specialists are subject matter experts who work with EdTech companies to ensure that educational content, such as textbooks, videos, or software, aligns with curriculum standards and educational best practices.
- Professional Development Coordinator: These professionals design and deliver technology-focused professional development programs for educators. They help teachers and staff learn how to effectively integrate EdTech tools into their classrooms and schools.
- EdTech Consultant: EdTech consultants provide expertise to educational institutions on selecting and implementing technology solutions that align with their goals and needs. They help schools and districts make informed decisions about adopting EdTech products and provide ongoing support.
- Product Manager (Education Domain): Product managers in the education domain oversee the development and improvement of EdTech products and platforms. They collaborate with education experts to ensure that products meet the specific needs of educators and students.
- Curriculum Developer: Curriculum developers with a technology focus design and adapt curricula to incorporate EdTech tools and resources. They create lesson plans that seamlessly integrate technology into the teaching and learning process.
- Educational Researcher: Educational researchers in EdTech companies conduct studies and evaluations to assess the impact and effectiveness of technology-based educational interventions. They use research findings to inform product development and instructional design.
- Data Analyst (Education): Data analysts in the education sector specialize in analyzing educational data collected from technology platforms. They work with educators to identify trends, measure learning outcomes, and make data-driven decisions to improve educational programs.
- User Experience (UX) Researcher (Education): UX researchers in the education field focus on understanding how students and educators interact with EdTech

products. They conduct user research to inform the design and usability of EdTech interfaces.

- Accessibility Specialist: Accessibility specialists in EdTech companies ensure that digital educational materials and platforms are accessible to all students, including those with disabilities. They work to comply with accessibility standards and guidelines.

These education-adjacent positions bridge the gap between educational expertise and technology implementation, helping EdTech companies create products and services that effectively support teaching and learning. Professionals in these roles play a vital role in ensuring that technology enhances, rather than hinders, the educational experience.

School-Facing Jobs

School-facing jobs in the EdTech sector involve working directly with K-12 schools, teachers, and students to implement, support, or promote EdTech solutions. These roles bridge the gap between technology providers and educational institutions, ensuring that technology is effectively integrated into the classroom. Here are some school-facing jobs in EdTech and their key responsibilities:

Title	Role	Responsibilities
EdTech Integration Specialist	Work directly with teachers and school staff to integrate technology into the curriculum.	• Provide training and professional development to educators. • Help teachers select and implement appropriate EdTech tools. • Support the integration of technology into lesson plans. • Collaborate with teachers to design engaging digital learning experiences.
EdTech Coach or Trainer	Train teachers and staff on how to use specific EdTech platforms or tools effectively.	• Conduct workshops and training sessions for educators. • Offer one-on-one coaching to teachers. • Troubleshoot technical issues and provide support. • Stay informed about updates and new features of EdTech tools.
Account Manager or Customer Success Manager	Build and maintain relationships with school clients to ensure successful adoption and use of EdTech products.	• Serve as a liaison between the EdTech company and schools. • Understand the unique needs of each school or district. • Provide ongoing support and guidance to school administrators and teachers. • Identify opportunities for product improvement based on school feedback.

Title	Role	Responsibilities
Sales Representative (K-12)	Promote and sell EdTech products to schools and districts.	• Prospect and reach out to potential school clients. • Conduct product demonstrations and presentations. • Understand school needs and tailor solutions. • Negotiate contracts and close sales deals.
EdTech Product Trainer	Specialize in training school clients on how to use a specific EdTech product effectively.	• Develop training materials and resources. • Deliver product training sessions to school staff. • Customize training based on school needs and goals. • Collect feedback and provide input for product improvement.
Educational Consultant (EdTech)	Offer expertise and guidance to schools on EdTech integration, curriculum design, and best practices.	• Assess school needs and goals for EdTech adoption. • Develop customized technology integration plans. • Provide ongoing support and recommendations. • Stay current with EdTech trends and innovations.

Title	Role	Responsibilities
Instructional Designer (EdTech)	Collaborate with EdTech companies to design effective and engaging learning materials and resources.	• Create digital learning content, such as courses and modules. • Ensure alignment with educational standards and best practices. • Conduct user testing and gather feedback for improvements. • Stay updated on pedagogical and technological advancements.
EdTech Content Specialist	Focus on curating and developing educational content for EdTech platforms.	• Curate and organize digital content for educators. • Collaborate with educators to create custom content. • Ensure content is age appropriate and aligned with curriculum standards. • Monitor content usage and effectiveness.

These school-facing roles in EdTech play a crucial role in helping schools and teachers leverage technology to enhance teaching and learning. They require a deep understanding of education, pedagogy, and technology to effectively support the integration of EdTech solutions in the classroom.

Being an Ambassador

Being an EdTech ambassador typically involves promoting and advocating for EdTech in educational settings. EdTech ambassadors are enthusiastic advocates for the effective use of technology in teaching and learning. They often work to bridge the gap between EdTech companies or providers and schools or educators, helping to facilitate successful implementation and adoption of technology solutions. Here's what it means to be an EdTech ambassador and how you can become one:

- Promotion: EdTech ambassadors actively promote the benefits of EdTech to educators, schools, and districts. They highlight how technology can enhance teaching and student outcomes.
- Advocacy: They advocate for the use of specific EdTech tools or platforms, sharing success stories and best practices with their peers.
- Professional Development: EdTech ambassadors often provide training and professional development to teachers and staff on how to effectively use technology in the classroom.
- Feedback: They serve as a bridge between educators and EdTech companies, providing valuable feedback on product usability, features, and improvements.
- Resource Sharing: Ambassadors share resources, lesson plans, and strategies for integrating technology into the curriculum.
- Networking: They connect with other educators, EdTech providers, and stakeholders in the education technology community to build a network of support and collaboration.

Now that you know the benefits of being an EdTech ambassador, here are the steps you could take to become one.

1 Share your Passion for EdTech: First and foremost, you should have a genuine passion for EdTech and a belief in its potential to transform education.
2 Develop Expertise: Develop expertise in the use of specific EdTech tools or platforms. Familiarize yourself with their features, capabilities, and best practices.
3 Gather Experience: Gain experience using EdTech in your own teaching or educational context. Implement EdTech solutions in your classroom and measure their impact.
4 Network: Attend conferences, workshops, and EdTech events to network with professionals in the field. Building connections can open doors to ambassador opportunities.
5 Collaborate: Collaborate with EdTech companies or providers that align with your educational goals and values. Many EdTech companies seek educators to serve as ambassadors or advocates.
6 Create Content: Share your expertise and experiences through blog posts, webinars, social media, and other channels. Create valuable content that showcases your knowledge and passion for EdTech.
7 Engage with Peers: Engage with other educators and school communities. Offer assistance, guidance, and support to colleagues who are looking to integrate technology.
8 Engage with Professional Learning: Stay updated on the latest trends and innovations in EdTech by participating in relevant professional development opportunities.
9 Apply for Ambassador Programs: Many EdTech companies and organizations have ambassador programs or advocacy initiatives. Look for opportunities to apply to become an official ambassador for a specific product or platform.
10 Build a Portfolio: Create a portfolio or resume that highlights your EdTech expertise, experiences, and contributions to the field. This can be useful when applying for ambassador roles.

11 Commit: Be prepared to commit time and effort to your ambassador role, including attending meetings, training sessions, and events.

Becoming an EdTech ambassador can be a fulfilling way to share your passion for EdTech, support your peers, and contribute to the integration of technology in education. It allows you to play a vital role in helping educators and schools harness the potential of EdTech for improved teaching and learning outcomes.

Joining an Advisory Committee/Council

Joining an EdTech advisory council or committee can be a valuable opportunity for educators to have a voice in shaping the development and implementation of EdTech tools and solutions. These advisory groups typically bring together educators, administrators, and experts to provide feedback and guidance to EdTech companies or organizations. I will say that you can try out being on a counsel without having to leave your position and you have a real opportunity to help grow a product or shape a company. As a current EdTech entrepreneur, we certainly appreciate when users have free accounts and agree to share their feedback and thoughts about what we are doing. When I was in the classroom, I served as both an ambassador as well as an advisor for several different tools. For me, it was an opportunity to weigh in and get the features I wanted that weren't available yet. Plus, I know my input positively impacted the tool and other educators benefited from my feedback.

Here's how educators can join such councils or committees and the benefits of doing so:

1 Research EdTech Companies: Identify EdTech companies or organizations whose products or initiatives align with your expertise and interests. Visit their websites and look for information about advisory councils or committees.

2 Reach Out: Contact the EdTech company's customer support or outreach team to express your interest in joining their advisory council. In some cases, they may have a formal application process. Provide your qualifications and explain why you're interested.

3 Networking: Attend EdTech conferences, webinars, and workshops to network with professionals in the field. Engage in conversations and express your interest in serving on advisory councils.

4 Connect on Social Media: Follow EdTech companies and professionals on social media platforms like LinkedIn and X. Engage in discussions and share your expertise. Companies may reach out to potential advisors through these platforms.

5 Professional Organizations: Join relevant professional organizations or associations in the EdTech field. These organizations often have connections with EdTech companies and may facilitate opportunities to serve on advisory boards.

6 Educator Communities: Join online educator communities and forums where EdTech topics are discussed. These platforms can be a source of information about advisory opportunities.

You may be asking yourself, why do I want to get involved in this capacity? Here are some benefits to being an ambassador or on an advisory council:

Influence: As a member of an advisory council, you have the opportunity to influence the design and development of EdTech tools and solutions. Your insights and feedback can shape products to better meet the needs of educators and students.

Professional Growth: Serving on an advisory council can be a valuable professional development opportunity. You'll gain a deeper understanding of the EdTech industry and trends, which can enhance your expertise as an educator.

Networking: You'll have the chance to network with professionals from both the education and technology sectors.

Building these connections can open doors to new opportunities and collaborations.

Access to Resources: EdTech companies often provide advisory council members with early access to new products, resources, and educational materials. This can be beneficial for your own teaching or professional development.

Advocacy: By participating in an advisory role, you become an advocate for effective technology integration in education. You can share your experiences and promote best practices among your peers.

Community Impact: Your involvement can contribute to the improvement of EdTech products, potentially benefiting educators and students on a larger scale. It allows you to make a positive impact on education.

Recognition: Serving on an advisory council can enhance your professional reputation and demonstrate your commitment to advancing education through technology.

Voice in Decision-Making: You'll have the opportunity to provide input on important decisions related to product features, usability, and educational outcomes.

Continual Learning: Being part of an advisory council keeps you updated on the latest EdTech developments, innovations, and research in the field.

Contributions to Education: Ultimately, your contributions can help create more effective and student-centered EdTech solutions that benefit the entire education community.

When joining an EdTech advisory council or committee, it's important to carefully consider the commitment involved and ensure that it aligns with your professional goals and interests. Your active participation and feedback can play a crucial role in improving the quality of EdTech and its impact on teaching and learning. Additionally, since this book is about shifting careers, I'd be remiss if I didn't speak about how being an ambassador or advisor offers opportunities to build relationships that can eventually turn into paid work. I know many folks who have shifted careers this way. They fall in love with the product while they are in the classroom, they evangelize for the product and then they formally get involved, and when they are ready to leave their current job they have a ready-made role to move into.

 Final Thoughts

Many of the folks I spoke to in EdTech, whether through the survey results or friends and colleagues who work in the industry in different ways, say the same thing. Often, relationships with companies start while you're in the classroom and you become an expert user of the tool. Perhaps you develop a relationship with your rep or other folks who work at the company and when you start questioning whether or not you want to stay in your teaching position, you have an established relationship to potentially move into a part or full-time job with that company. As you're considering your own personal skill set and how you'd like to spend your time, consider the following reflection questions.

 REFLECTION QUESTIONS

- What tools have you enjoyed using while in your current or former positions?
- What kind of technology tools do you gravitate toward? Do you have a contact at that company already?
- Once you've shortlisted which companies or tools you may be interested in, have you visited their website and see if they have an advisory team or an ambassador program?
- Can a part-time position help you acquire some skills that will make you more qualified for a future position somewhere else?

8 Publishing

Whether you are an educator who taught about writing or media, or a person who enjoys sharing ideas, publishing may be the right move for you. You don't have to be the best writer; you must be a great communicator. In today's climate, you can find a niche area you can grow into, and anything is possible as long as you have a passion for it. Folks with areas of expertise can create content of their own that can be the launch pad for a career as a consultant or a speaker. This chapter is going to be more about the different kinds of publishing, formats and ideas about what the specific platforms can offer, and how to get involved with each. When I get to the publishing roles at the end, that will explore more positions and how your skills may line up with each job type.

Another idea to consider is that any of the electronic modes of sharing content (podcast, blog, vlog, etc.) can be something you do on the side as you are building your audience and later can be leveraged for revenue. There are many sponsors who are willing to pay for air space on your content once it proves to be well read or listened to. Many free blog sites, for example, will have ads already appearing on your blog to offset your free account. This is a big topic to cover and I don't want to get in the weeds, so I recommend that if you'd like to leverage your personal blog, vlog, or podcast for

 DOI: 10.4324/9781003450702-9

income you can check out these sites or any of the many other sites if you just search Google:

- www.wix.com/blog/how-to-make-money-blogging
- https://riverside.fm/blog/how-to-make-money-podcasting

Podcasting

Starting a podcast can be an exciting way to share your expertise, stories, or content with a wider audience. Podcasting, if you don't know what it is, is like a recorded radio show. It's usually an audio opportunity for conversations or sharing ideas of your own. However, many of the new platforms that are available now for recording and hosting podcasts allow for video as well. There are lots of podcasts out there already and you can find them on Apple podcast, Spotify, or other platforms. One of my favorite education podcasts is Cult of Pedagogy hosted by Jennifer Gonzalez and her team. She also has a blog branded with the same name that has become quite popular. Jenn was a teacher before starting this venture that was a hobby at first, and now it is a money-making venture. I also have a podcast that my company sponsors called Building Learner-Centered Spaces and we focus on ways to build inclusive learner-centered classrooms. Our guests have shared so many resources and ideas for helping educators. Additionally, the Teach Better Podcast Network that we are a part of has a great many podcasts worth listening to. Networking in this way offers a variety of benefits that may help a new podcast. Here's a step-by-step guide to help you get started.

1 Define Your Podcast's Niche: Choose a specific topic or theme for your podcast. It could be related to education, a hobby, storytelling, interviews, or anything you're passionate about. You can do some research on what's out there. Which podcasts do you enjoy and what about them is enjoyable? If you're going to pick a topic that is saturated, how will your angle be different?

2 Planning and Content Creation: Outline episode topics, create scripts, or plan discussions to ensure your content is organized and engaging.

3 Choose Equipment: Invest in quality podcasting equipment, including a microphone, headphones, and recording software. You can start with a basic setup and upgrade as needed.

4 Recording: Find a quiet space to record your episodes. Use recording software (e.g., Audacity, Adobe Audition) to capture clear audio.

5 Editing: Edit your episodes to remove any mistakes, pauses, or background noise. Add intro/outro music, transitions, and effects if desired.

6 Hosting Platform: Choose a podcast hosting platform (e.g., Anchor, Libsyn, Podbean) to store and distribute your podcast episodes to various podcast directories.

7 Create Artwork and Description: Design podcast artwork and write a compelling description that reflects your podcast's content and style.

8 Submit to Directories: Submit your podcast to major directories like Apple Podcasts, Spotify, Google Podcasts, and more.

9 Promotion: Share your podcast on social media, your website, and relevant online communities. Encourage listeners to subscribe and leave reviews.

Remember that podcasts require consistency, quality content, and engagement with your audience. It's normal to improve over time, so don't be discouraged if your initial episodes or videos aren't perfect and don't get very many listeners. The key is to enjoy the process and connect with your audience authentically and don't give up if it doesn't take off right away. It's normal to only have a few listeners at first, but inviting the right guests with different networks than your own is a good way to spread the word.

Blogging

When you decide to blog, it can be as formal or informal as you like. Remember that your voice and narrative matter, so there is no one right way to do it. I have written a whole book called *Blogging for Educators* (2015) about how teachers can start blogging and why it is important we do. Telling classroom educator stories is so important to help folks understand the work we do and this is one way we can control our own narratives instead of letting the media drive public opinion about our profession.

Blogging is a written digital opportunity to share information, stories, and tips to readers. There are many different platforms you can blog on that offer free or paid versions like WordPress or Wix. These are just examples as I'm reluctant to add too many because they change frequently. For example, some of the platforms mentioned in my 2015 book no longer exist. What you need to know is that blogs are places to share ideas and invite conversation via comments and social media. Blogging is essentially what introduced my work to the world. Since anyone can blog, it gives you a forum to share ideas without the gatekeeping of more formal publication. This doesn't mean you should rant and rave on your blog, but rather look at it as a way to communicate on the topics that you think are important.

Using your blog can be an opportunity to get your name out there and share your expertise. If you're successful with your blog, then it can also be a springboard for future more formal publication. In fact, my work with my blog and guest blogging for Peter DeWitt is what made it possible for me to write the book about blogging. It was the relationship I cultivated with Peter and his knowledge of my writing that created the opportunity for me to be a part of the Connected Educator series with Corwin. Not to mention the fact that my blog with *Ed Week* put me in the public eye.

In the next section you will read about vlogging, which is essentially the same as blogging except the format is video instead of writing. On your written blog it is easy enough to embed video, but vlogging is straight up video with a short description that utilizes keywords so that you can be found in online searches.

Vlogging

Vlogging, like blogging, offers a good way to share content that can help your target audience. If you're the kind of person who loves to create video content, then this is definitely the right space for you. YouTube is one place many folks vlog, and you can record your video or you can go live; it is free to start and syncs with your Google account. There are also revenue-generating opportunities when your channel gets enough subscribers. Here is how you can get started with vlogging:

1 Choose Your Vlog's Focus: Decide what kind of content you'll create – educational videos, personal vlogs, tutorials, travel, or any other topic that interests you.
2 Content Planning: Plan your video content, including topics, formats, and any scripts or outlines you'll use.
3 Equipment and Setup: Invest in a good camera, microphone, and lighting to ensure high-quality video and audio. Find a well-lit and quiet place to record.
4 Recording and Editing: Record your vlog footage and use video editing software (e.g., Adobe Premiere Pro, Final Cut Pro) to edit your videos.
5 Video Hosting Platform: Upload your vlogs to video hosting platforms like YouTube or Vimeo. Create a channel and optimize titles, descriptions, and tags.
6 Engaging Thumbnails and Titles: Design eye-catching thumbnails and craft descriptive and engaging video titles.
7 Promotion: Share your vlogs on social media, your website, and relevant online communities. Engage with viewers' comments and encourage subscriptions.
8 Consistency and Engagement: Publish videos regularly to keep your audience engaged. Respond to comments and feedback to build a community.

Books

It seems like everyone is writing books these days in education and why not? One of my first publications catapulted me into a world of other opportunities. Writing a book is a chance to demonstrate your expertise while helping others solve problems that are a part of their everyday work. Or if you choose to write something other than an education book, it can be something that entertains readers. When I started writing, I did short work on my blog, but as a writing instructor I thought it was important to demonstrate my own expertise to show my students that I was doing the things I was suggesting to them. When you work with seniors, this level of transparency is really important. My students really responded to knowing that I was a published author and that I actively practiced all of the techniques I recommended they use. Additionally, a momentum builds once you write your first book, and other opportunities are more likely to start happening.

My first book, *Simply May*, a historical fiction novel, began as a short story I was writing as a model for my 9th grade students. While they wrote their stories, I wrote mine. They liked mine so much, they insisted I needed to finish it. I did and I self-published it after I hired an editor to review and provide feedback. This book was just a way for me to show myself I could do it. Most people aren't even aware that I wrote this book. My second book was called *Teaching Mythology Exposed*, which was also self-published. I did a lot of research for that book and leveraged my growing social media network to ensure that my assumptions about early career teaching matched what pre-service teachers feared and worried about. It was through this research that I made long-lasting relationships with professors who teach pre-service teachers, and I continue to volunteer to work with them. It was with this second book that I got my big break. I had the opportunity to moderate a #Satchat on a Saturday morning as I mentioned in the social media chapter. It was here that I met Peter DeWitt and that changed everything.

My experience with writing books is not typical for everyone, but that doesn't mean it can't happen that way for you. My third book was my first published book by a big publisher, Corwin, in the Connected Educator series. From my *Education Week Teacher* blog, I got a book offer from Rowman and Littlefield to write about questioning and so I did. Then I made connections with people at ASCD at a conference when they attended a session I presented on reflection and I wrote my first book about reflection with ASCD called *Teach Students to Self-Assess*. Next came *Hacking Assessment* because of my connection with Mark Barnes, whom I met through the Connected Educator series, and the list goes on. It's not hard to see how the dominos start to line up and fall when you get yourself in the right space to be visible and you have expertise to share.

If you have a book idea, there are many ways to get started in publishing. I'm happy to talk to you about the pros and cons of the various publishing companies. Most of them have both pros and cons; it is just a matter of what you are hoping to achieve by publishing. Are you interested in making a higher royalty or reaching a wider audience, or do you have niche idea that will be better served by a smaller press that specializes in your area? Only you can make this decision. There are a lot of publishers out there, big and small, and they all have something to offer. Do your research, ask the questions, and make sure that you at least put together an annotated table of contents (TOC) and write at least one chapter, especially if you have never been published before.

Developmental Editing

Being a developmental editor is a lot like being a writing teacher or coach. As a matter of fact, what I enjoyed most about my role as a developmental editor was my work directly with authors. It wasn't unlike my time with students as I was helping them develop their own voices. My role as an editor in this capacity was to be a reader and to be curious. How could I best help this writer communicate their ideas in a way that readers will understand?

Transitioning from being an English teacher to becoming a developmental editor for a publishing house is a viable career path, as your skills in language, literature, and communication are highly relevant to the field of editing and publishing. Here are steps to help you make this transition:

1 Build Relevant Skills and Knowledge: While teaching English provides a strong foundation, consider taking additional courses or workshops in editing, publishing, and writing. Familiarize yourself with style guides (e.g., Chicago Manual of Style) and publishing industry standards.

2 Create a Portfolio: Start building a portfolio of your editing work. You can begin by offering your editing services to friends, colleagues, or local writers to gain experience. Document your editing projects and showcase them in your portfolio.

3 Network: Attend publishing-related events, conferences, and workshops to network with professionals in the industry. Join writing and editing associations, such as the Editorial Freelancers Association (EFA) or the American Society of Journalists and Authors (ASJA), to connect with potential clients and employers.

4 Develop an Online Presence: Create an online presence as a freelance editor. Build a website or use platforms like LinkedIn or professional editing networks to showcase your skills and attract potential clients or employers.

5 Market Yourself: Highlight your teaching experience as an asset in the editorial field. Emphasize your ability to analyze and critique writing, provide constructive feedback, and communicate effectively.

6 Gain Experience: Look for freelance or part-time editing opportunities, especially in educational or academic publishing. These roles often value teaching experience and familiarity with educational content.

7 Publish: Consider applying for positions in educational publishing, such as textbook development or educational

content creation. Your teaching experience can be particularly valuable in these roles.

8   Participate in Professional Development: Continue your professional development by staying updated on industry trends, attending workshops, and expanding your knowledge of different publishing niches (e.g., fiction, non-fiction, academic, children's books).

9   Apply for Positions: Start applying for developmental editor positions at publishing houses, literary agencies, or freelance editing firms. Tailor your resume and cover letter to emphasize your teaching background and editing skills.

10 Prepare to Interview: Prepare for interviews by researching the specific publishing house, understanding their genres or niches, and demonstrating your ability to provide valuable developmental input on manuscripts.

11 Freelance: If you prefer freelance work, market your services to authors, self-publishers, and small presses. Showcase your expertise in helping writers develop their manuscripts.

12 Build a Reputation: Reputation is vital in the editing world. Deliver high-quality work, meet deadlines, and maintain professionalism to build a positive reputation in the industry.

13 Feedback and Continuous Improvement: Be open to feedback from authors, clients, or colleagues, and use it to continuously improve your editing skills.

Transitioning from teaching to developmental editing may take time, but your background in English and education can provide a strong foundation for success in this field. As you gain experience and build your reputation, you'll be well positioned for a fulfilling career as a developmental editor in the publishing industry. Of course, you don't have to be an English teacher to be a good candidate for this kind of job; you just have to love writing and help others improve their voice. It helps if you have a good understanding of the language and writing mechanics. Being a reader is helpful too.

Running a Publishing Company

Becoming a publisher involves establishing a company or platform that produces and distributes books, magazines, digital content, or other materials to a target audience. Publishing is a multifaceted endeavor that requires careful planning, industry knowledge, and effective business strategies. During COVID-19, I had the privilege of running Mimi and Todd Press. This was a new endeavor for me, and it was daunting because there wasn't much I knew about doing it aside from what I learned being a writer working with a lot of different publishers. But one thing I knew well is how I wanted to treat authors and the kind of experience I wanted them to have when they worked with us. I wanted them to feel like they trusted us with their important work. Although the work wasn't ultimately for me, I'm glad I spent a couple of years doing it. Here are the steps to become a publisher:

1   Educate Yourself: Familiarize yourself with the publishing industry, including its trends, challenges, and different types of publishing (e.g., traditional, self-publishing, digital).
2   Define Your Niche and Focus: Determine the type of content you want to publish (e.g., fiction, non-fiction, educational, magazines) and identify your target audience.
3   Business Plan: Create a comprehensive business plan that outlines your publishing goals, strategies, budget, revenue projections, and marketing plans.
4   Choose a Business Model: Decide whether you want to focus on traditional publishing (working with authors and agents) or self-publishing (providing publishing services to authors).
5   Legal Considerations: Register your publishing business as a legal entity (e.g., LLC, corporation) and obtain any necessary licenses or permits.
6   Secure Funding: Determine how you'll fund your publishing venture, whether through personal savings, investors, loans, or grants.

7   Acquire ISBNs: If you're publishing books, obtain International Standard Book Numbers (ISBNs) for each title. These unique identifiers are essential for distribution and sales tracking.

8   Build a Team: Assemble a team of professionals, which may include editors, designers, marketers, salespeople, and distribution experts.

9   Content Acquisition: Acquire content through various means, including working with authors, commissioning writers, or curating submissions.

10 Editing and Proofreading: Ensure the content you acquire is professionally edited and proofread to maintain quality.

11 Design and Formatting: Design covers and format interiors for printed books and digital publications.

12 Production: Convert manuscripts into print-ready files or digital formats, depending on your publishing model.

13 Distribution Channels: Decide how you'll distribute your publications, whether through traditional bookstores, online platforms, or direct sales.

14 Marketing and Promotion: Develop a marketing strategy to promote your publications through online and offline channels, including social media, advertising, and author events.

15 Sales and Revenue Generation: Establish relationships with retailers, online marketplaces, and distributors to ensure your publications reach your target audience.

16 Rights Management: If you're acquiring content, establish clear terms and agreements regarding rights and royalties with authors or contributors.

17 Publish and Launch: Publish your titles according to your publishing schedule and launch them with a coordinated marketing effort.

18 Monitor Performance: Continuously track sales, reader feedback, and market trends to adapt your publishing strategies.

19 Adapt and Grow: Be prepared to adapt to changes in the industry and explore opportunities for growth and expansion.

Becoming a publisher requires a combination of business acumen, industry knowledge, and a passion for bringing valuable content to your audience. It's important to approach the process with dedication, professionalism, and a commitment to delivering high-quality publications. If this is something you are truly interested in, it is important to get started working in the industry, so you can learn a lot of the necessary sector jargon from the work you will be doing.

Curriculum Development

Writing curriculum for an education company or publisher is a multifaceted process that involves careful planning, content development, alignment with educational standards, and quality assurance. Curriculum writers play a crucial role in creating educational materials that meet the needs of students and teachers. Here are the key steps and considerations involved in writing curriculum for an education company or publisher:

Needs Assessment and Research:

- Begin by conducting a needs assessment to understand the target audience, such as grade levels, subject areas, and educational goals.
- Research educational trends, best practices, and the specific requirements of the curriculum project.
- If possible, discuss the goals of the project with the people that you are creating the curriculum for. What do they have already? What kinds of issues have they had in the past? What is the focus of the content?

Alignment with Standards:

- Ensure that the curriculum aligns with relevant educational standards, such as Common Core State Standards, state standards, or international frameworks.
- Select priority standards when creating alignment.
- Make sure to create a cross-walk for educators to see and understand the alignment at a glance.

Curriculum Design and Structure:

- Determine the overall structure and scope of the curriculum, including the sequence of lessons, units, and learning objectives.
- Create a curriculum framework or outline that outlines the content, assessments, and instructional strategies.
- Research the structure of other curricula and ensure that any issues from past iterations don't exist this time.

Content Development:

- Develop instructional content, including lesson plans, activities, templates, assessments, and teaching materials.
- Write clear, engaging, culturally responsive, and age-appropriate content that supports the curriculum's learning objectives.

Differentiation and Inclusivity:

- Consider the diverse needs of learners and incorporate differentiation strategies to address various learning styles, abilities, and backgrounds.
- Ensure that the curriculum is inclusive and accessible to all students, including those with disabilities.

Assessment and Evaluation:

- Develop formative and summative assessments that align with the curriculum's learning outcomes.
- Include rubrics and scoring guidelines to help teachers evaluate student performance.

Technology Integration:

- If applicable, incorporate technology tools, digital resources, and online platforms to enhance the curriculum's effectiveness.

Teacher Support Materials:

- Create teacher guides, answer keys, and support materials that assist educators in implementing the curriculum effectively.
- Offer professional development resources to help teachers understand the curriculum's goals and strategies.

Quality Assurance:

- Review and revise the curriculum materials to ensure accuracy, clarity, and alignment with standards.
- Conduct pilot testing and gather feedback from educators to refine the curriculum.

Graphic Design and Layout:

- Collaborate with graphic designers and layout specialists to format the curriculum materials, making them visually appealing and user-friendly.

Editorial Review:

- Conduct thorough proofreading and editorial reviews to eliminate errors in grammar, spelling, and content.
- Ensure that the language used is age appropriate and engaging for students.

Legal and Copyright Considerations:

- Verify that all content is copyright compliant and adheres to intellectual property laws.
- Address any legal and ethical considerations related to educational materials.

Publication and Distribution:

- Prepare the curriculum for publication, which may include printing physical copies or making digital versions available for download.

- Plan the distribution strategy to make the curriculum accessible to schools, teachers, or educational institutions.

Feedback and Updates:

- Continuously gather feedback from educators and students to make necessary updates and improvements to the curriculum.
- Stay informed about changes in educational standards and adapt the curriculum accordingly.

Training and Professional Development:

- Provide training and professional development opportunities for teachers and educators to effectively implement the curriculum.

Writing curriculum for an education company or publisher requires a collaborative approach that involves educators, subject matter experts, instructional designers, editors, and curriculum developers. The goal is to create high-quality educational materials that support effective teaching and learning. Having been an educator makes you uniquely qualified to do this as you have likely used a variety of different curricula and know what worked for your kids.

 Final Thoughts

So I'm sure you've noticed in this chapter that there is a lot of overlap content wise for the different platforms you might choose, but the way you deliver or share your content would be different depending on how you share it. It's about knowing what media works best for you and how to showcase the work you want to share or how to help others showcase their work. If you're interested in the backend side of things, working in design or marketing could also offer a venue to be a part of this work that is different from what you may be used to already.

REFLECTION QUESTIONS

- What content do you want to share?
- What is your strength? Writing? Speaking? Editing? Video editing?
- Which format most intrigues you?
- Do you already have a blog, vlog, or podcast? If yes, do you want to grow it or leverage what you have started? Where will you start?
- Do you have an idea for a book? If yes, have you researched to see if anyone else has written about your topic already? When? How will your book be different?
- If you have published before, what did you like best about the experience? What would you change?

9 Social Media

Social media is a broad and evolving space that has created another digital way to communicate, connect, and share content and build relationships. In many ways, it is the new advertising platform that has forced every educator to consider the way they present themselves in the world. It turns out these tools also give educators and students power to communicate in ways that haven't always been easy or readily available to anyone mostly for free.

As a journalism teacher in the classroom, social media was starting to emerge as a new way to tell stories both for me as a teacher and writer and for my student journalists to tell stories. I realized quickly that if I was going to truly prepare students for a career in journalism, I needed to learn about the platforms, how to use them, and how to be responsible on all of them. Meeting students where they were on this was an essential part of my learning these important skills. Ultimately, my use of these tools also expanded my imagination about possibilities, and it turned out that I quite liked using the tools for many different reasons and I became proficient quickly in communicating with my audience in this way. Teachers who effectively know how to use social media can parlay those skills into lucrative positions. As a matter of fact, my ability to use these tools aided in my obtaining a high-visibility blog on *Education Week Teacher*, which led to several other writing opportunities, and I also served as a social media manager for ECET2, a project that the Bill and

    DOI:10.4324/9781003450702-10

Melinda Gates Foundation created to celebrate teachers and teaching. I'm sure you noticed the job on my resume in the second chapter.

Platforms That Support Education

When I was in the classroom, the outlets I was most accustomed to using were Twitter, Facebook, Instagram, WordPress, LinkedIn, and Periscope. Obviously a lot has changed since I was first learning these platforms. There have been other platforms that have come and gone and those I have listed have changed or were acquired, and the overall feel of some communities has changed. The nature of social platforms is that they are ever evolving with the technology and the networks. It is because of this that I'm not going to go into too much detail about this here. I'll just mention that you should be aware of what is current now and how you can leverage it for branding and potential future work. My job as a social media manager couldn't have happened without what I learned from my journalism classes, and I don't have a classic background in art and advertising, so I was definitely learning on the job.

Personal Branding

Personal branding is the practice of creating and managing a distinct professional identity and reputation for yourself. It involves showcasing your unique skills, expertise, values, and personality to establish a strong presence in your field or industry. For educators looking to build a business, personal branding can help differentiate you from others, attract potential clients or students, and establish credibility and trust. Here are steps educators can take to brand themselves for business:

Define Your Niche and Expertise:
- Identify your specific area of expertise within education. Are you a math tutor, a language learning expert, a college admissions coach, or a homeschooling consultant? Define your niche to target a specific audience.

Craft Your Unique Value Proposition:

- Determine what sets you apart from others in your niche. Highlight your unique skills, teaching methods, or qualifications that make you the right choice for your target audience.

Develop a Brand Persona:

- Think about the image you want to project. Consider your values, personality, and how you want others to perceive you. Your brand persona should be authentic and relatable to your audience.

Create a Professional Online Presence:

- Build a professional website or blog that showcases your expertise, services, and testimonials from satisfied students or clients.
- Maintain active and professional social media profiles, especially on platforms where your target audience is active.

Consistent Branding Elements:

- Use consistent branding elements such as a professional logo, color scheme, and visual style across your website, social media, and marketing materials.

Content Marketing:

- Share valuable content related to your field through blog posts, articles, videos, or webinars. Position yourself as an authority by providing helpful and insightful information.

Engage with Your Audience:

- Interact with your audience through comments, messages, and discussions. Respond promptly to inquiries and show that you value their input.

Networking and Collaboration:

- Build relationships with other educators, educational organizations, and influencers in your field. Collaborate on projects, guest post on each other's blogs, or participate in joint ventures.

Testimonials and Recommendations:

- Encourage satisfied students or clients to provide testimonials and recommendations that you can display on your website and marketing materials.

Offer Free Resources or Samples:
- Provide free resources, such as e-books, sample lessons, or webinars, to demonstrate your expertise and attract potential customers.

Market Yourself Effectively:
- Invest in targeted online advertising or marketing campaigns to reach your ideal audience. Use platforms like Google Ads, Facebook Ads, or LinkedIn Ads.
- Iterate on your plan as you see what is most effective. Finding the right keywords and demographic to target will help with effectiveness.

Continual Learning and Growth:
- Stay updated with the latest trends, research, and best practices in your field. Continuous learning enhances your expertise and credibility.

Collect and Analyze Data:
- Use analytics tools to track the performance of your online presence and marketing efforts. Adjust your strategy based on data insights.

Build Trust and Credibility:
- Consistently deliver high-quality services and maintain ethical standards to build trust and credibility with your students or clients.

Remember that personal branding is an ongoing process. It takes time to establish yourself as an authority and gain recognition. Be patient and persistent in building a successful education-focused business through personal branding.

Messaging and Marketing

Effective messaging as an educator involves clear and compelling communication of your value proposition. Whether you are promoting your work in your classroom, school, or district or the new book you just wrote, creating the right messaging will help you communicate what and to whom you want. Here are some elements of good messaging:

- Clarity: Clearly articulate your skills, experiences, and aspirations in a way that is easy for others to understand.
- Relevance: Tailor your messaging to the needs and expectations of your target audience, whether it's potential employers, clients, or colleagues.
- Impact: Highlight your achievements and your positive impact in your previous role as an educator.
- Passion: Convey your enthusiasm and passion for your new career path, as it can be infectious and persuasive.
- Solutions-Oriented: Show how your skills and experiences can address challenges or provide solutions in your chosen field.
- Authenticity: Be true to yourself and your experiences. Authenticity builds trust and credibility.
- Storytelling: Share stories and examples illustrating your capabilities and accomplishments.
- Value Proposition: Clearly state what you bring to the table and how it benefits your audience.
- Adaptability: Emphasize your ability to adapt and learn quickly, showcasing your versatility.
- Professionalism: Maintain a professional tone and demeanor in all your interactions and messaging.

Marketing yourself as a former educator involves highlighting your skills, expertise, and experiences to position yourself effectively for new career opportunities. Here are some steps and tips for marketing yourself as a former educator:

1 Identify Transferable Skills: Reflect on the skills you've gained as an educator that apply to other roles. These might include communication, problem-solving, leadership, adaptability, and organization.
2 Define Your Career Goals: Determine your career path or industry in which you want to transition. This will guide your messaging and marketing efforts.

3 Craft Your Brand: Develop a clear and compelling personal brand statement summarizing who you are, what you've accomplished as an educator, and how your skills can benefit your target audience.

4 Update Your Resume and LinkedIn Profile: Tailor your resume and LinkedIn profile to highlight your transferable skills and achievements as an educator. Use keywords relevant to your new career goals.

5 Network Effectively: Leverage your professional network and expand it to include contacts in your target industry. Attend industry events, join relevant associations, and participate in online networking groups.

6 Gain Relevant Experience: If possible, gain additional experience or qualifications related to your new career path. This might include taking courses, volunteering, or pursuing freelance opportunities.

7 Develop a Portfolio: Create a portfolio that showcases your skills and accomplishments. Include examples of lesson plans, instructional materials, student achievements, or any relevant projects you've worked on.

8 Craft a Compelling Elevator Pitch: Develop a concise elevator pitch explaining your educational background and why you're a valuable asset in your new career field.

9 Demonstrate Adaptability: Emphasize your ability to adapt to new challenges and environments. Highlight instances where you've successfully transitioned or taken on new roles in your educational career.

10 Highlight Soft Skills: Soft skills like empathy, patience, communication, and collaboration are highly valued in many industries. Showcase your proficiency in these areas.

11 Be Authentic: Authenticity is key to effective messaging. Be genuine about your experiences and aspirations, and communicate your passion and enthusiasm for your new career path.

12 Tailor Your Applications: Customize your cover letters, applications, and interview responses to show how your educator experience directly relates to the specific role you're applying for.

13 Seek Guidance and Mentorship: Connect with mentors or career coaches who can guide and advise on your transition.

14 Practice Self-Marketing: Share your journey and experiences on social media or through a personal blog. This can help raise your profile and attract opportunities. You are not pushy for sharing your story and you deserve to share it. Imposter syndrome is real, but that doesn't mean you aren't qualified. In fact, your story matters to us and we want you to share it. If it helps even just one person, then it was worth it.

15 Leverage Testimonials and Recommendations: If you have received positive feedback or recommendations from colleagues, supervisors, or students, use them to reinforce your qualifications.

16 Be Patient and Persistent: Transitioning to a new career may take time. Be patient and persistent in your efforts, and don't be discouraged by setbacks or rejections.

Remember that marketing yourself as a former educator is about presenting yourself in the best possible light while staying true to your skills and experiences. It's effectively communicating your unique value to potential employers or clients in your new career path and leveraging that to move through opportunities that will satisfy your intellectual needs.

Networking

I know we discussed networking opportunities to find a new job in Chapter 2, but in this context, networking is more about getting the word out about the work you are doing now. Networking is a recurring theme really in every chapter as it is how ideas spread and there are lots of ways to do it. 50 years ago, advertisers didn't have the same opportunities since the internet wasn't ubiquitous yet. Social media is a powerful tool that we can use to show our authentic selves, connect with like-minded individuals, and showcase our offerings. I recommend that you sign up for a few platforms, start following people you admire, and take notes on what you notice. This could be a great starting point for getting involved in the right conversation that changes your trajectory.

Developing a Website

Websites are an essential part of how interested parties find us when we are sharing content. Once I wrote my first book, it was important to have a place that my audience could go to access more of my work or to connect with me if they wanted me to come speak or work with their schools. Ultimately, it also became a place that was a portfolio for my career since it has a blog, my speaking gigs, and a variety of testimonials that provide credibility for what I charge people to work with me. I strongly recommend building a website and if you can't do it yourself, it is worthwhile to hire someone to do it for you. It was a frustrating experience for me once I moved from WordPress to Wix, and I eventually hired a professional to take what I did and make it better.

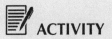 **ACTIVITY**

Before you build a website of your own, I recommend that you visit other websites of people who do what you want to do. Make a list of different websites you like and ones you don't like as much. What do you like about the ones you chose? How might you emulate what you see on your own website? What don't you like about the websites you've selected? How can you avoid those qualities? This activity will help you get ideas for color themes, fonts, and usability that can make or break the user experience.

Remember that setting up a website to market yourself as an educator is an effective way to showcase your expertise, share resources, and connect with students, parents, and colleagues. Here are the steps to help you create a professional educator website:

Define Your Purpose and Goals:

- Determine the main objectives of your website. Are you using it to share teaching resources, promote your tutoring services, or provide information about your expertise and experience?

Choose a Domain Name:

- Select a domain name that reflects your identity as an educator and is easy to remember. You can use domain registrars like GoDaddy or Namecheap to purchase a domain.
  Select a Website Hosting Platform:
- Choose a website hosting platform that suits your needs. Popular options for educators include WordPress, Wix, Squarespace, and Weebly. Each platform has its own features and ease of use.

Choose a Website Template or Theme:

- Select a website template or theme that aligns with your goals and vision for your site. Most website builders offer a range of professionally designed templates.

Customize Your Website:

- Customize the template to create a unique and visually appealing website. Personalize the color scheme, fonts, and layout to match your branding.

Create Essential Pages:

- Build key pages for your website, including:
  - Home Page: Introduce yourself and provide an overview of your expertise and services.

- About Page: Share your professional background, qualifications, and teaching philosophy.
- Services or Offerings Page: Describe the educational services you provide, whether it's tutoring, coaching, or consulting.
- Blog or Resource Page: If you plan to share educational content, create a blog or resource page to post articles, lesson plans, or guides.
- Contact Page: Include a contact form or contact information for inquiries.
- Testimonials Page: Display endorsements and reviews from satisfied students, clients, or colleagues.
- Portfolio or Projects Page: Showcase your past work, projects, or accomplishments.

Organize Your Content:

- Arrange your content in a logical and user-friendly manner. Use clear navigation menus to help visitors find information easily.

Optimize for SEO:

- Implement basic search engine optimization (SEO) practices to improve your website's visibility in search engines. Use relevant keywords, optimize images, and create descriptive meta tags.

Integrate Social Media and Sharing Buttons:

- Include social media icons and sharing buttons to encourage visitors to follow you on social platforms and share your content.

Add Contact Information:

- Provide multiple ways for visitors to contact you, including a contact form, email address, and possibly a phone number (if you're comfortable sharing it).

Set Up Analytics:

- Install website analytics tools like Google Analytics to track visitor behavior, traffic sources, and other valuable data.

Test and Review:

- Thoroughly test your website's functionality, including links, forms, and multimedia elements. Review the content for accuracy and clarity.

Launch Your Website:

- Once you're satisfied with your website, publish it for the world to see. Promote your website on your social media profiles and among your professional network.

Regularly Update and Maintain:

- Keep your website up to date by adding fresh content, updating information, and addressing any technical issues that arise.

Promote Your Website:

- Use your website's URL in your email signature, on your business cards, and in any promotional materials. Share your website on social media and encourage others to do the same.

Monitor and Improve:

- Continually monitor the performance of your website and seek feedback from visitors. Make improvements and adjustments based on user behavior and feedback.

Remember to respect privacy and security considerations when sharing content related to your students or educational institution, and adhere to any relevant privacy policies and regulations. Your website is a valuable tool for personal branding and professional growth as an educator and the likely place people who are looking for you will go. Make sure that when people Google you, your website appears near the top of the search. You want to decrease any barriers to people wanting to work with you.

 Final Thoughts

20 years ago, social media didn't exist in the capacity that it does now, but it is safe to say that it is here to stay. Rather than declare that you aren't interested in getting onto social platforms or engaging in conversation about conspiracy theories (yes, I have worked with educators who believe that the government tracks you once you go on social media), find a way to leverage these important tools to get your name out there. Aside from making yourself visible in the place where most people start their searches, you will have many opportunities to meet, collaborate with, and grow as a professional through the connections you meet online. Believe it or not, Connie Hamilton and I met on Twitter and now she is one of my best friends. We started out as professional colleagues, then became co-authors when writing *Hacking Homework*, and now she is like family. You just don't know who you will meet or what opportunity will come your way when you get things moving online. Start small, choose a network you feel comfortable in, and grow from there. I can't wait to see you. You can follow me on X (formerly Twitter) @MsSackstein, on LinkedIn – make sure to message me and tell me you read this book, on Facebook @Starr Sackstein, NBCT, and on Instagram @Starr53177. See you soon.

REFLECTION QUESTIONS

- How comfortable are you with online social platforms? Which ones are you currently on? How many followers do you have?
- If you aren't comfortable, what is keeping you from trying out a social platform?
- How can you overcome the challenges you have to be successful using social media?
- How can you create a website that emulates the ones you liked?
- Have you started to gather content to put on the website? Where do you have gaps that you need to fill?
- What books or articles have you read to support your effort to move into this space?

10 School Law and Policy

Positively influencing education doesn't only happen in classrooms and schools. An educator with an interest in advocacy or educational reform can get involved with the legal side of education. Whether you decide to work to shift education policy federally, by state or hyperlocally, you have the power and the knowledge to effect important change on a broader scale.

After I settled into the classroom a few years in and started getting involved in assessment and grading reform, I used to joke with my students that when I grow up, I want to work for a lobby group to change the way we do assessment nationally. It is my greatest desire to help rid our educational system of standardized tests and grades for all kids. No matter how long I'm in education, I believe it is my calling to make permanent change. In this chapter you will learn more about how to get involved with different kinds of jobs that work on law and/or policy. There are many different ways to get involved, and these options are just scratching the surface.

Parent Advocacy

As a teacher who worked in a school with a high percentage of recently immigrated families, we often were challenged by a lack of appropriate communication to support students. I want to be clear that this wasn't because parents weren't interested or were negligent; often they were disenfranchised because they didn't have good experiences in their home countries or they are fearful of public institutions for a variety of reasons. These families would have been excellent candidates for parental advocacy.

A parent advocate in education is an individual who works to support and advocate for the educational rights and needs of students, often their own children or other students in their community. Parent advocates play a vital role in ensuring that students receive a quality education, access necessary services and accommodations, and are treated fairly within the educational system. Here's an overview of what a parent advocate in education does and how you can become one:

Roles and Responsibilities of a Parent Advocate in Education:

- Supporting Their Child: Parent advocates often start by advocating for their own children. This may involve attending Individualized Education Program (IEP) meetings, communicating with teachers and school administrators, and ensuring that their child's educational needs are met.
- Navigating the Education System: Parent advocates help families navigate the complexities of the education system, including understanding special education laws (e.g., IDEA) and regulations, as well as school policies and procedures.
- Ensuring Educational Rights: Advocates work to ensure that students' rights are protected and that they receive appropriate educational services and accommodations. This may include advocating for students with disabilities, English language learners, or students facing discrimination.
- Collaborating with Schools: Parent advocates collaborate with teachers, school staff, and administrators to create positive educational experiences for students. They foster open communication and problem-solving.
- Attending Meetings and Workshops: Advocates may attend workshops, training sessions, and meetings related to education laws and policies to stay informed and build their advocacy skills.

School Law and Policy

- Raising Awareness: Advocates raise awareness about education issues in their community and may advocate for systemic changes to improve educational quality and equity.

Steps to Become a Parent Advocate in Education:

1   Understand Education Laws: Start by gaining a solid understanding of education laws, regulations, and policies that pertain to your area of interest, such as special education, civil rights, or general education policies. You can do this by researching online, attending workshops, or seeking guidance from experts in the field.

2   Network and Connect: Connect with other parent advocates, local education organizations, and support groups. Networking can help you learn from experienced advocates and access valuable resources.

3   Build Your Knowledge: Continue to educate yourself about education issues, advocacy techniques, and relevant resources. Stay informed about the latest developments in education policy and practice.

4   Advocate for Your Child: Begin by advocating for your own child within the educational system. Attend meetings, communicate with teachers, and actively participate in your child's education.

5   Volunteer: Offer your time and expertise to local education-related organizations, parent–teacher associations, or advocacy groups. Volunteering can provide valuable experience and connections.

6   Seek Training and Resources: Look for advocacy training programs, workshops, and online courses that can help you build your advocacy skills and knowledge. Some organizations offer specialized training for parent advocates.

7   Get Involved: Attend school board meetings, parent–teacher association meetings, and other educational gatherings to engage with your community and stay informed about local education issues.

8   Advocate for Others: Once you have gained experience and knowledge, consider extending your advocacy

beyond your own child by assisting other families who may need support and guidance.

9 Join Advocacy Organizations: Consider joining advocacy organizations focused on education issues, such as the National Parent Teacher Association (PTA), Council of Parent Attorneys and Advocates (COPAA), or local grassroots groups.

10 Stay Informed and Updated: Education laws and policies can change, so it's essential to stay informed and adapt your advocacy efforts accordingly.

Becoming a parent advocate in education can be a fulfilling way to make a positive impact on the educational experiences of students and the overall quality of education in your community. Your advocacy can help ensure that all students have access to the resources and support they need to succeed.

Student Advocacy

Legal student advocacy in education involves the legal representation and support of students in educational matters, with the goal of ensuring that students' rights are protected and that they have access to a fair and equitable education. This field of advocacy can cover a wide range of issues and situations, and it typically involves legal professionals, such as attorneys or advocates, who specialize in education law. Here are some key aspects of legal student advocacy in education:

Special Education Advocacy: Special education advocates work on behalf of students with disabilities to ensure they receive appropriate educational services and accommodations as mandated by the Individuals with Disabilities Education Act (IDEA). They may assist with Individualized Education Program (IEP) development, placement decisions, and dispute resolution.

Discipline and Due Process: Legal advocates may represent students facing disciplinary actions, including suspensions or expulsions, and help ensure that the school follows due process procedures, respects the student's rights, and provides a fair hearing.

Civil Rights and Discrimination: Advocates may address cases of discrimination, harassment, or civil rights violations in schools, including issues related to race, gender, sexual orientation, religion, or national origin. They may file complaints with appropriate agencies or pursue legal action when necessary.

Access to Education: Advocates can assist students in securing access to education when barriers exist, such as issues related to enrollment, transportation, or language access for English language learners.

Bullying and Harassment: Advocates may work to address bullying and harassment in schools, ensuring that schools have policies and procedures in place to prevent and respond to such incidents and representing students who have been victimized.

School Funding and Resource Equity: Legal advocates may be involved in litigation related to school funding and resource allocation, particularly in cases where disparities in funding result in educational inequalities.

Education Policy and Reform: Some legal advocates work on broader education policy issues, advocating for systemic changes that promote equity and access to quality education for all students.

Student Records and Privacy: Advocates help students and their families understand and protect their rights concerning the confidentiality of educational records under the Family Educational Rights and Privacy Act (FERPA).

College and Higher Education Advocacy: In higher education, legal advocates can assist students with issues related to admissions, financial aid, academic accommodations, and disciplinary matters at colleges and universities.

Alternative Education Options: Advocates may help families explore alternative education options, such as homeschooling or charter schools, and navigate the legal requirements associated with these choices.

Legal Representation in Court: In some cases, legal advocates may represent students in court, either in administrative hearings or in civil litigation, to protect their rights and interests.

Advocacy within Schools: Some advocates work within schools and educational institutions, advising administrators, teachers, and students on compliance with education laws and regulations.

Legal student advocacy in education requires a deep understanding of federal and state education laws, as well as the ability to navigate legal procedures and advocate effectively on behalf of students. Legal advocates often work closely with families, educators, school administrators, and relevant government agencies to resolve disputes and ensure that students' rights are upheld in educational settings.

You can find some resources for family advocacy in the appendix.

Local School Boards

Getting involved in your local school board is one way to stay connected to education even if you aren't in a classroom anymore, and it can it help you continue to make the impact you may crave.

Running for a local school board is a significant commitment that can impact your community's education system. If you're an educator interested in running for a school board position, here are the steps you can take:

1   Eligibility Check: Review the eligibility requirements for school board candidates in your district. These requirements may include residency, voter registration, and other criteria. Ensure you meet these requirements.
2   Understand the Role: Familiarize yourself with the responsibilities and duties of school board members. Attend school board meetings to gain a better understanding of how the board operates.
3   Formulate a Vision: Develop a clear vision for what you hope to achieve as a school board member. Identify

specific goals and priorities that align with your passion for education and your community's needs.

4 Build a Campaign Team: Assemble a team of volunteers to help with your campaign. This team may include campaign managers, fundraisers, communicators, and grassroots organizers.

5 Campaign Financing: Create a budget for your campaign and establish a fundraising strategy. School board campaigns can vary in size and funding needs, so it's important to plan accordingly.

6 Collect Signatures: Depending on your district's requirements, you may need to collect a certain number of signatures from registered voters to qualify for the ballot. Familiarize yourself with the petitioning process and deadlines.

7 File Necessary Paperwork: Submit all required paperwork, including candidacy filings and financial disclosures, by the specified deadlines. Comply with all election rules and regulations that are required for your particular state as they can vary from state to state, district to district.

8 Campaign Strategy: Develop a comprehensive campaign strategy that includes outreach, messaging, and voter engagement. Create a campaign website, social media profiles, and campaign materials to convey your platform.

9 Engage with the Community: Attend local events, meetings, and forums to engage with voters and discuss your vision for education. Be accessible and responsive to community members' questions and concerns.

10 Educate Yourself: Stay informed about the issues facing your school district and the broader education landscape. This will help you articulate informed positions and solutions.

11 Debate and Public Forums: Participate in candidate debates and public forums to present your ideas and engage in discussions with other candidates and voters.

12 Campaign Ethics: Conduct your campaign with integrity and adhere to ethical standards. Avoid negative

campaigning and focus on your qualifications and vision for the district.

13 Get Out the Vote: Mobilize your supporters to vote on Election Day. Encourage community members to participate in the democratic process.

14 Comply with Reporting Requirements: Ensure that you follow all campaign finance reporting requirements, including disclosing campaign contributions and expenditures.

15 Election Day: Be present at polling places, if allowed, to greet voters and answer any last-minute questions. Encourage your supporters to vote.

16 Post-Election: Whether you win or lose, continue to engage with your community on education issues. If you are elected, be prepared to transition into your role as a school board member.

Remember that running for a school board position requires dedication, time, and effort. It's essential to maintain a positive and respectful campaign, as you will be representing your community's interests in education policy and decision-making if you are elected.

Lobby Groups

Education lobby groups are organizations that advocate for specific policies, reforms, or interests related to education. These groups often work to influence lawmakers, policymakers, and the public to support their agendas. Here are some well-known education lobby groups in the United States:

Organization	Description	Website
National Education Association (NEA)	The NEA is one of the largest teachers' unions in the United States. It advocates for educators and public education funding while also promoting policies that support teachers and students.	www.nea.org
American Federation of Teachers (AFT)	Similar to the NEA, the AFT is a prominent teachers' union that advocates for educators and students. It focuses on issues such as teacher rights, school funding, and education quality.	www.aft.org
National Parent Teacher Association (PTA)	The National PTA is a grassroots organization that brings together parents, teachers, and students to advocate for policies that benefit children and improve education.	www.pta.org
Council for Exceptional Children (CEC)	CEC is a professional organization that advocates for individuals with disabilities and special education. It works to ensure that students with exceptionalities receive appropriate services and support.	https:// exceptionalchildren. org
National School Boards Association (NSBA)	The NSBA represents school board members and advocates for public education policies at the local, state, and federal levels.	www.nsba.org

Organization	Description	Website
Association of American Colleges and Universities	AAC&U focuses on higher education and advocates for initiatives that enhance the quality of undergraduate education, promote liberal education, and advance student learning outcomes.	www.aacu.org
National Association of Independent Schools (NAIS)	NAIS represents independent (private) schools and promotes the interests of these schools, as well as advocating for the value of independent education.	www.nais.org
EdTrust	The Education Trust is a non-profit organization that works to close educational achievement gaps and improve educational equity, with a particular focus on underserved student populations.	https://edtrust.org
Alliance for Excellent Education	This organization advocates for policies and practices that improve high school graduation rates and prepare students for success in college and careers.	https://all4ed.org
Stand for Children	Stand for Children is a non-profit organization that focuses on ensuring that all children, regardless of their background, have access to a high-quality education.	https://stand.org

These are just a few examples of education lobby groups in the United States. Many other organizations exist at the local, state, and national levels, each with its own specific areas of focus and policy priorities. Additionally, other countries have their own education advocacy organizations that work to influence education policies and practices within their respective contexts.

Educators who are interested in getting involved in education lobby groups can take several steps to become active participants and advocates for education policy and reform. Here's a general guide on how educators can get involved:

1 Research and Identify Relevant Organizations: Start by researching education lobby groups that align with your interests and values. Consider whether you want to focus on specific issues, such as teacher rights, curriculum development, special education, or broader education policy.

2 Join Professional Associations: Many educators are members of professional organizations related to their field, such as the National Education Association (NEA) or the American Federation of Teachers (AFT). These organizations often have lobbying arms and provide opportunities for members to engage in advocacy.

3 Attend Meetings and Conferences: Attend meetings, conferences, and events organized by education lobby groups. These gatherings provide opportunities to learn about current issues, network with like-minded individuals, and connect with leaders in the field.

4 Volunteer for Campaigns: Education lobby groups frequently run advocacy campaigns aimed at promoting specific policies or reforms. Consider volunteering your time to support these campaigns by making phone calls, sending emails, or participating in rallies and marches.

5 Advocate Locally: Lobbying and advocacy efforts often start at the local level. Attend school board meetings, city council meetings, and state legislative sessions to voice your concerns and advocate for education policies that benefit students and educators.

6   Engage in Social Media and Online Advocacy: Follow education lobby groups on social media platforms to stay informed about their activities and policy priorities. Share relevant information with your network and engage in online advocacy efforts.

7   Contribute to Research and Policy Development: If you have expertise in a specific area of education, consider contributing to research or policy development efforts within an organization. Your knowledge and experience can be valuable in shaping effective education policies.

8   Write Letters and Op-Eds: Craft letters to elected officials and write op-eds or articles for local newspapers or education-focused publications to express your views on important education issues.

9   Build Relationships with Legislators: Develop relationships with your elected representatives, both at the state and federal levels. Schedule meetings with them to discuss your concerns and the policies you support.

10 Support Fundraising Efforts: Many education lobby groups rely on donations and fundraising to support their advocacy work. Consider making financial contributions to organizations you believe in.

11 Run for Office: Some educators choose to take their advocacy efforts to the next level by running for school board positions or other elected offices that influence education policy.

12 Stay Informed: Continuously educate yourself on education issues, policy changes, and research findings. Being well informed strengthens your advocacy efforts.

Remember that education lobby groups often have different approaches and priorities, so it's important to find one that aligns with your values and goals. Additionally, be aware of any legal restrictions or ethical guidelines that may apply to educators' involvement in advocacy, especially if you work in a public school or government-funded institution.

Working with an education lobby group can offer several benefits to educators who are passionate about improving education policies and practices. Here are some of the advantages:

- Influence Policy: Education lobby groups are often at the forefront of advocating for policies and reforms that can positively impact education. By working with these organizations, educators can play a direct role in shaping policies that affect their classrooms and students.
- Amplify Your Voice: Lobby groups provide a platform for educators to amplify their voices on important issues. They offer opportunities to express concerns and advocate for changes at local, state, and national levels.
- Networking Opportunities: Joining an education lobby group allows educators to connect with like-minded individuals who share their passion for education. Networking can lead to valuable collaborations, partnerships, and support systems.
- Access to Resources: Many education lobby groups provide resources, research, and information to help educators stay informed about current education issues and best practices. These resources can be valuable for improving teaching methods and curriculum.
- Professional Development: Some education lobby groups offer training and professional development opportunities for educators interested in advocacy and leadership roles. These programs can enhance educators' skills and knowledge.
- Advocacy Training: Lobby groups often provide training on effective advocacy techniques, including how to communicate with policymakers, build public support, and make a persuasive case for education policies.
- Policy Impact: Through education lobby groups, educators can contribute to meaningful changes in education policy, funding, and legislation. Their advocacy efforts can lead to improvements in student outcomes, teacher working conditions, and the overall education system.
- Unity and Collective Action: Education lobby groups bring together educators, parents, and other stakeholders who are passionate about education. By working collectively, advocates can have a stronger impact than they would as individuals.

- Recognition and Awards: Some education lobby groups recognize outstanding contributions to education advocacy with awards and honors, which can enhance an educator's professional reputation.
- Influence on Educational Equity: Many education lobby groups prioritize issues of educational equity and access. Educators working with these groups can contribute to efforts to reduce achievement gaps and ensure that all students have access to a high-quality education.
- Personal Growth: Engaging in advocacy can lead to personal growth and development. It can help educators build leadership skills, gain confidence in public speaking, and develop a deeper understanding of education policy issues.
- Positive Change: Ultimately, the most significant benefit of working with an education lobby group is the opportunity to be part of positive change in education. Advocates can see their efforts lead to improvements in educational outcomes and opportunities for students.

It's important for educators to carefully consider which education lobby group aligns with their values and goals and to be aware of any legal or ethical considerations related to their involvement, especially if they work in public education settings.

Non-profit Organizations

Starting a non-profit organization involves several key steps to establish a legal entity dedicated to a specific charitable, educational, or social cause. Here's a general guide on how to start a non-profit:

1 Define Your Mission and Purpose: Clearly define the mission and purpose of your non-profit. Identify the specific issue you aim to address and the goals you intend to achieve.

2 Research and Planning: Research existing organizations in your field to ensure that your non-profit's mission is unique and fills a gap. Develop a comprehensive business plan outlining your goals, strategies, target audience, programs, and anticipated outcomes.

3 Choose a Name: Select a unique and meaningful name for your non-profit that reflects its mission. Check the availability of the chosen name and ensure it's not already in use by another organization.

4 Form a Board of Directors: Assemble a diverse and committed board of directors. Board members provide governance, strategic direction, and oversight to the organization.

5 Draft Bylaws: Create the bylaws that outline the internal rules and operating procedures of your non-profit. This document should cover areas such as membership, board structure, decision-making processes, and meetings.

6 Incorporate Your Non-Profit: File the necessary incorporation documents with the appropriate state agency. This typically involves submitting articles of incorporation, which outline your non-profit's purpose and structure.

7 Apply for Tax-Exempt Status: To qualify for tax-exempt status under section 501(c)(3) of the Internal Revenue Code (for charitable organizations), you need to apply for recognition from the IRS. This involves submitting Form 1023 or the streamlined Form 1023-EZ.

8 Develop a Fundraising Plan: Outline your non-profit's fundraising strategies. This could include grants, donations, events, memberships, and other fundraising activities.

9 Open a Bank Account: Open a bank account in your non-profit's name. This account will be used to manage financial transactions related to the organization.

10 File Necessary State and Local Paperwork: Depending on your location and the nature of your non-profit, you may need to file additional paperwork at the state and local levels. This could include obtaining licenses or permits.

11 Create Policies and Procedures: Develop policies and procedures that govern various aspects of your non-profit's operations, such as financial management,

conflict of interest, volunteer engagement, and program implementation.

12 Build a Strong Brand: Create a visual identity for your non-profit, including a logo, website, and marketing materials. Establish a strong online presence to promote your mission and attract supporters.

13 Recruit Volunteers and Staff: Start recruiting volunteers and staff members who are passionate about your cause and can help you implement your programs and initiatives.

14 Launch Your Programs: Begin implementing your programs and initiatives to achieve the goals outlined in your business plan. Continuously evaluate and adjust your programs as needed.

15 Maintain Compliance: Regularly file required reports with the IRS and other relevant government agencies to maintain your non-profit's tax-exempt status. Comply with all legal and regulatory requirements.

Starting a non-profit is a complex process that requires careful planning, legal compliance, and dedication. Consider seeking legal advice and consulting resources provided by organizations that support non-profit startups to ensure that you follow all necessary steps.

State Education

Jobs in state education agencies encompass a wide range of roles dedicated to overseeing and improving the education system within a specific state or territory in the United States. These agencies are responsible for implementing state education policies, ensuring compliance with federal laws, and supporting local school districts and schools. Here are some common jobs in state education agencies and the qualifications typically required for these roles.

Title	Qualifications
State Education Commissioner or Superintendent	Typically, candidates for this top leadership position should have a strong background in education, often with a master's or doctoral degree in education leadership or a related field. Extensive experience in education administration and policy is usually required, along with proven leadership abilities.
Deputy or Assistant Commissioner	Similar to the commissioner or superintendent, individuals in these positions typically have advanced degrees in education or a related field and significant experience in education administration and policy.
Program Director or Manager	Program directors and managers often have master's degrees in education or a related field, along with several years of experience in program management and education policy.
Education Policy Analyst	A bachelor's or master's degree in education, public policy, or a related field is often required. Policy analysts should have strong analytical and research skills.
Curriculum Specialist	A bachelor's or master's degree in education, curriculum development, or a related field is typically required. Curriculum specialists should have teaching experience and expertise in instructional design.

Title	Qualifications
Education Data Analyst	A bachelor's or master's degree in data analysis, statistics, education, or a related field is usually required. Proficiency in data analysis software and strong analytical skills are essential.
School Improvement Specialist	Typically, a master's degree in education or a related field is preferred. Experience as an educator or in school leadership roles is often necessary. Knowledge of school improvement strategies is crucial.
Education Outreach Coordinator	A bachelor's degree in education, communications, or a related field is common. Strong communication and outreach skills, as well as an understanding of education policies, are important.
Grant Manager or Specialist	A bachelor's or master's degree in finance, business, or a related field is often required. Experience in grant management or administration is typically necessary.
Education Researcher	A master's or doctoral degree in education research, statistics, or a related field is usually required. Strong research skills, including data collection and analysis, are essential.
Legislative Liaison or Government Affairs Specialist	A bachelor's or master's degree in political science, public policy, or a related field is common. Strong advocacy and communication skills, as well as knowledge of the legislative process, are important.

Title	Qualifications
Special Education Coordinator	A master's degree in special education or a related field is often required. Special education coordinators should have teaching and administrative experience in special education programs.
Human Resources Manager	A bachelor's or master's degree in human resources, business administration, or a related field is typically required. HR certifications and experience in HR management are important.

These qualifications are general guidelines, and specific requirements can vary by state and agency. State education agencies often seek candidates with a strong commitment to education, a deep understanding of education policies, and the ability to work collaboratively with diverse stakeholders. Additionally, some positions may require specific certifications or licenses, such as teaching or administrator licenses, depending on their responsibilities. It's important to check the job listings and requirements of the specific state education agency you are interested in to ensure you meet the qualifications for the desired role.

Federal Education

Federal education agencies in the United States play a crucial role in developing education policies, distributing federal funding, and ensuring compliance with federal laws. These agencies offer various job opportunities for individuals interested in contributing to the improvement of the nation's education system. Here are some common jobs in federal education agencies and the qualifications typically required for these roles.

Title	Qualifications
U.S. Secretary of Education	The U.S. Secretary of Education is a Cabinet-level position appointed by the President and confirmed by the Senate. The Secretary typically has a strong background in education, policy, or a related field, along with significant leadership experience.
Deputy Secretary of Education	Similar to the Secretary, the Deputy Secretary often has advanced degrees in education or a related field and extensive experience in education leadership and policy.
Education Policy Analyst	A bachelor's or master's degree in education, public policy, or a related field is often required. Policy analysts should have strong analytical and research skills.
Program Specialist or Manager	Program specialists typically have a bachelor's or master's degree in education, public administration, or a related field. Several years of experience in program management and education policy may be required.
Education Researcher or Statistician	Research roles often require a master's or doctoral degree in education research, statistics, or a related field. Strong research and data analysis skills are essential.
Education Outreach Coordinator	A bachelor's degree in education, communications, or a related field is common. Strong communication and outreach skills, as well as an understanding of education policies, are important.

Title	Qualifications
Legislative Affairs Specialist or Government Relations Coordinator	A bachelor's or master's degree in political science, public policy, or a related field is often required. Strong advocacy and communication skills, as well as knowledge of the legislative process, are important.
Grant Manager or Specialist	A bachelor's or master's degree in finance, business, or a related field is typically required. Experience in grant management or administration is often necessary.
Education Program Evaluator	A bachelor's or master's degree in education evaluation, research, or a related field is common. Experience in program evaluation and data analysis is important.
Education Technology Specialist	A bachelor's or master's degree in educational technology, instructional design, or a related field is often required. Knowledge of education technology trends and tools is essential.
Human Resources Manager	A bachelor's or master's degree in human resources, business administration, or a related field is typically required. HR certifications and experience in HR management are important.
Foreign Language Specialist	Specialists in this role often have advanced degrees in foreign languages, linguistics, or language education. Proficiency in multiple languages may be required.

Title	Qualifications
Special Education Specialist	Special education specialists typically have master's degrees in special education or a related field. Experience in special education programs and knowledge of federal special education laws (e.g., IDEA) are essential.
Attorney or Legal Advisor	Legal roles often require a Juris Doctor (JD) degree and state bar admission. Experience in education law, administrative law, or related areas is important.
Public Affairs Specialist or Communications Specialist	A bachelor's or master's degree in communications, public relations, or a related field is common. Strong communication and media relations skills are essential.

Qualifications for federal education agency jobs can vary depending on the specific position and agency. However, most roles require a commitment to education, a deep understanding of education policies and regulations, and the ability to work effectively within a federal bureaucracy. Additionally, some positions may require security clearances or specialized certifications based on the nature of the work and agency. It's important to review the job listings and requirements for the specific federal education agency and position you are interested in to ensure you meet the qualifications.

✅ Final Thoughts

There are many ways you can stay engaged in education, as discussed in this chapter. Your experience doesn't have to end once your tenure in the classroom or in school leadership ends. Some of us have always believed that we are destined to do more for education beyond our hyperlocal experiences.

Regardless of how or where you seek your future steps, there are ways to make positive change that your experience will certainly support. We all have different, albeit similar at times, experiences in the school system and all of the groups mentioned in this chapter can benefit from your knowledge.

 REFLECTION QUESTIONS

- What do you value most in education and where might the best forum be for sharing those values?
- Are there specific areas of education you feel especially passionate about that you'd like to support?
- What areas of education can your experience aid in changing?
- How will you go about getting involved with this organization?
- What barriers might you have to overcome to be successful?
- What are your greatest hopes with getting involved in one of these groups?
- Have you created an educator philosophy statement? If not, this may help you focus on your passions and help you narrow your search.

11 Leaving a Legacy

Early in my career, I decided that if this was going to be the career I was going to work in, I was going to be the absolute best version of myself because I wanted to be a teacher that all kids remembered as the one who made a difference. Eagerly I connected with students in meaningful ways, working hard to be more than just a purveyor of knowledge.

Know Your Impact

Recently I wrote an article for *EL Magazine* about knowing our impact. It is often hard to see when we are in the middle of our careers. Sometimes we are judged or we judge ourselves based on the titles we hold or we are limited by those positions. I know that at the beginning of my career, the only impact that mattered to me was the direct effect of my teaching on the students I shared a space with. It was a tangible impact that was easy to see, track, and shift when and where I needed to. When I shifted into leadership, my impact was also felt in a different way through the teachers and their practices and now I have the opportunity to influence many through my publications and my consultancy work. I visit more schools in more places and present all over the world. It is because of this that the important ideas about student-centered learning are spreading globally.

 DOI: 10.4324/9781003450702-12

As you go into the world, away from your current job, keep in mind that no matter what you choose to do, you matter. Take comfort in this fact.

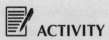
ACTIVITY

As you're coming to the end of this text, I'd like you to reflect on your impact. Consider the many jobs you've had, the students and/or educators you've spent your time with. Brainstorm a list of accomplishments you've already made. What would you still like to achieve?

Time to Pivot Again?

Regardless of what career path you choose, it is unlikely that you will stay with the same job or path for your entire adult life. Long are the days past where folks found the perfect career and job and then started and ended their careers in the same place. As a matter of fact, education may be the last harbinger of this phenomenon. With the world changing as it has over the last few decades, there is far more flexibility in how and what we do for work. So we are in a unique place in time where following a path or a journey can lead us in strange and sometimes mysterious ways. So if you find yourself antsy after being at a job for any amount of time, perhaps it is time to revisit the chart from Chapter 1. Are you experiencing any familiar or not familiar signposts that are helping you make decisions to move on? Only you can answer this question.

It's remarkable that our situation in life changes so much based on where we live if we decide to get married or divorced, or have children, or become empty nesters. When our circumstances change, so do our needs and, therefore, now may be the time to start considering other kinds of work or going back to the familiar. Or maybe you are financially independent now and can afford to volunteer or become an entrepreneur. It is possible that perhaps you have discovered a new problem that you have a solution for, and now you want to pursue creating that solution. It's amazing the kind of impact we can have once we have a little distance from the day to day and want to pursue other venues for helping educators, families, and systems.

No matter what your change of circumstance is, this could be another opportunity to take a different path at this new fork in the road. Hopefully by now, you have stopped labeling yourself based on job titles and have realized that you are able to pivot regardless of where you are in your career.

Time to Retire?

Deciding when to retire is a significant life decision that can be influenced by various personal, financial, and emotional factors. While the right time to retire varies from person to person, here are some common signs that it might be time to consider retirement:

1   Financial Preparedness: Assess your financial situation to determine if you have saved enough for retirement. Consider factors such as your retirement savings, pension, investments, and any other sources of income you'll rely on during retirement.
2   Health and Well-being: Your physical and mental health play a crucial role in retirement decisions. If your health is deteriorating or you're finding it challenging to cope with the demands of your job, it might be a sign to consider retirement.
3   Career Satisfaction: Reflect on your job satisfaction. If you're no longer finding fulfillment in your work, have accomplished your professional goals, or are feeling burnt out, it could be a signal that it's time to move on.
4   Family and Lifestyle: Consider your family's needs and your desired lifestyle during retirement. If you want to spend more time with family, travel, or engage in hobbies, retiring might align with your goals.

5 Workload and Stress: If the stress and workload of your job are taking a toll on your physical and mental health, it could be an indication that retirement would offer a better quality of life.

6 Work–Life Balance: If your job is preventing you from maintaining a healthy work–life balance, retirement might allow you to focus more on personal interests and well-being.

7 Age and Retirement Benefits: Evaluate your age and the retirement benefits offered by your employer or government. Some retirement plans have specific age criteria for full benefits or incentives to retire at certain ages.

8 Transition Planning: Consider whether your workplace has a succession plan in place and if you have a suitable successor. A well-planned transition can make the retirement process smoother.

9 Personal Goals: Reflect on your personal goals and aspirations. If you have dreams you want to pursue or experiences you want to enjoy during retirement, it might be the right time to retire.

10 Readiness for Change: Assess your readiness to transition from a work-focused routine to a more leisurely and self-directed lifestyle.

11 Social Connections: Consider the social connections and relationships you have outside of work. Retirement can impact your daily interactions, so evaluate whether you have a strong support network.

12 Work Opportunities: If you're interested in pursuing other opportunities, such as consulting, part-time work, or a different career path, retiring from your current job might open up these possibilities.

It's important to note that retirement is a deeply personal decision, and there is no one-size-fits-all answer. Take time to reflect on your individual circumstances, consult with financial advisors, consider your emotional well-being, and discuss your plans with loved ones. If possible, ease into retirement gradually, perhaps by reducing your work hours or responsibilities to help ensure a smoother transition. And always remember that even if you retire, it doesn't mean that you can't still work in a different career or volunteer. Personally, I know that I wouldn't do well with retirement, but that doesn't mean that I wouldn't grow into it when the time is right. If it is right for you, you've earned it! Be proud.

Mentorship

Mentorship is a professional relationship in which an experienced and knowledgeable individual (the mentor) provides guidance, support, and advice to another person (the mentee) who is typically less experienced or knowledgeable in a particular field or domain. Mentorship entails several key elements like knowledge transfer where the mentor shares their expertise, knowledge, and experience with the mentee. This may involve teaching specific skills, providing insights into the field, and offering guidance on professional development. And we all know that when new folks start, they are never as ready as they need to be to feel successful. Mentors can bolster confidence and provide support and encouragement. The mentor offers emotional support, encouragement, and motivation to the mentee. This support helps boost the mentee's confidence and resilience in facing challenges.

Additionally, as a mentor, you can provide guidance and critical feedback. You can provide guidance on setting goals, making decisions, and navigating career or educational paths. Mentors offer constructive feedback on the mentee's performance and areas for improvement. If you have the luxury of being in the school with the teachers, then you can visit their classes and provide very specific feedback relating to what you see and their goals without the worry of evaluation that may come with the same duties from a supervisor.

Think of the role models from your career. What did you love about them? Were you fortunate enough to have a mentor of your own? What did you learn from them? Mentors serve as role models, demonstrating professionalism, ethical behavior, and best practices in the field. Mentees can learn by observing their mentor's actions and values and engaging in important discourse. Remember to ask questions, be vulnerable, and allow your mentor to help show you the way. When you share your challenges with your mentor, they can help you problem solve. Mentors assist mentees in problem-solving and decision-making. They help mentees identify solutions to challenges and make informed choices. They also help with personalized guidance because of the relationships they develop with you and the people they know in their networks that can also make a more robust experience. We have to be able to lean on our mentors – this could be your opportunity to help newbies the way you were lucky to be helped in the beginning. Make sure to pay it forward.

Mentorship is a long-term commitment, and the duration of the mentorship relationship can vary. It may last for several months or extend over several years, depending on the goals and needs of the mentee. I can speak from experience that different mentors have helped me over the years. My first mentor helped me navigate the school I was in and what to expect as she was a veteran teacher in my building. The other ones I've had over the years have been so helpful in many different ways – especially as a sounding board, building mutual respect, and having challenging conversations that helped me consider my decisions and grow from things I didn't know.

Mentorship can take various forms, including one-on-one mentoring, group mentoring, formal mentorship programs, and informal mentorship relationships. It is common in fields such as education, business, healthcare, science, and the arts, among others.

The goals of mentorship can vary widely, from professional skill development and career advancement to personal growth and leadership development. Ultimately, mentorship is a collaborative and supportive relationship that benefits both the mentor and the mentee. The mentor gains satisfaction from helping others succeed, while the mentee receives valuable guidance and support on their journey toward personal and professional goals.

Veteran educators have a wealth of experience and knowledge that can be highly valuable to newer teachers. Getting involved in mentorship allows veteran educators to share their expertise, support the professional development of their colleagues, and contribute positively to the education community. Here are some steps for veteran educators to get involved in mentorship:

1 Identify Your Mentorship Goals: Consider what you hope to achieve through mentorship. Are you interested in mentoring new teachers, helping colleagues advance in their careers, or providing specialized guidance in a particular area (e.g., classroom management, curriculum development)? Define your objectives.

2 Express Your Interest: Let your school or district administration know that you're interested in mentoring. They can help connect you with teachers who could benefit from your guidance.

3 Participate in Mentorship Programs: Many schools and districts have formal mentorship programs in place. Inquire about these programs and express your interest in becoming a mentor.

4 Offer Peer Support: Be open to informal mentoring relationships. Reach out to colleagues who may benefit from your expertise and offer your assistance.

5 Stay Current: Keep your knowledge and skills up to date. Continuous professional development ensures that you're providing the most relevant and effective guidance to mentees.

6 Attend Workshops and Training: Participate in mentorship training programs or workshops offered by your school or district. These sessions can provide valuable insights into effective mentoring practices.

7 Establish Boundaries: Clearly define the scope and limits of your mentorship role. Ensure that both you and your mentee understand expectations, goals, and time commitments.

8 Listen Actively: Effective mentors are good listeners. Take the time to understand your mentee's needs, challenges, and goals. Provide guidance and support tailored to their individual circumstances.

9. Set Clear Objectives: Work with your mentee to set clear, achievable goals. These objectives can guide your mentorship sessions and help measure progress.

10 Provide Constructive Feedback: Offer constructive feedback and guidance in a supportive manner. Help your mentee identify areas for improvement and suggest strategies for growth.

11 Share Resources: Share educational resources, lesson plans, books, and articles that may be beneficial to your mentee's professional development.

12 Model Best Practices: Lead by example. Demonstrate effective teaching methods, classroom management techniques, and professional conduct that your mentee can learn from.

13 Celebrate Successes: Acknowledge and celebrate your mentee's achievements, no matter how small. Positive reinforcement can boost confidence and motivation.

14 Maintain Confidentiality: Respect the confidentiality of your mentee's concerns and issues. Create a safe and trusting environment for open dialogue. This is especially helpful in environments that may be fraught with a "gotcha" mentality. Teachers are often wary of help they receive unless they are the ones actively seeking you out.

15 Reflect and Adapt: Periodically reflect on your mentorship experiences and make adjustments as needed. Adapt your mentoring approach to meet the evolving needs of your mentee.

16 Seek Feedback: Encourage your mentee to provide feedback about your mentoring style and the support they receive. Use this feedback to improve your mentorship practices.

17 Stay Committed: Mentorship is an ongoing commitment. Be consistent and reliable in your support for your mentee.

18 Advocate for Mentorship: Promote the value of mentorship within your school or district. Encourage other

veteran educators to become mentors and share the benefits of mentorship with administrators. It could be useful to get testimonials from the educators you work with and start a blog sharing resources.

Getting involved in mentorship as a veteran educator not only benefits your mentees but also enriches your own professional journey. It allows you to give back to the education community, make a positive impact on colleagues' careers, and contribute to the growth and development of future generations of educators.

Volunteerism

Retired teachers have a wealth of knowledge and experience that can be incredibly valuable to their communities. Getting involved in volunteerism after retirement is a meaningful way to continue making a positive impact. Firstly, volunteer and work in tutoring and mentoring. Educators can offer their expertise by volunteering as tutors or mentors for students in need. Many schools, libraries, and community organizations have tutoring programs where retired teachers can help students with their academic challenges. But it doesn't have to be limited to students; veteran teachers can help other educators and people in many areas of their lives. If you are more interested in working with adults, you can consider volunteering at adult education centers or community colleges to assist adults in improving their literacy, numeracy, or language skills. Your teaching experience can be a valuable asset in adult education settings. To this end, senior education programs are also a good option. Share your knowledge with fellow retirees by leading educational workshops or classes at senior centers or retirement communities. Topics could include history, literature, art, or any subject you're passionate about.

Some other places that may be available for volunteering are listed below:

Non-profit Organizations	Many non-profit organizations, especially those focused on education and youth development, welcome retired teachers as volunteers. You can help with program planning, curriculum development, and mentoring.
Library Programs	Volunteer at your local library to support literacy initiatives, reading programs, or library events. Libraries often appreciate volunteers who can assist with organizing and promoting educational activities.
Online Tutoring	Consider offering your tutoring services online through platforms that connect educators with students in need. This allows you to reach a broader audience and work from home.
School Committees	Join school committees or advisory boards to provide your insights and expertise on educational matters. Your perspective as a retired educator can be valuable in shaping school policies and programs.
Community Workshops	Organize or lead workshops on education-related topics in your community. This could include parent workshops, study skills sessions, or teacher professional development sessions.
Literacy Programs	Volunteer with literacy organizations or programs that promote reading and literacy among children and adults. You can assist with literacy assessments, reading events, and book drives.

Cultural Institutions	Museums, science centers, and cultural institutions often welcome volunteers to help with educational programs and exhibits. Your background in education can enhance visitors' experiences.
Online Courses	Consider creating online courses or educational content on platforms like Udemy, Coursera, or Teachable. This allows you to share your knowledge and earn income or donate proceeds to a charity of your choice.
International Volunteering	Explore opportunities for international volunteer work in education. Some organizations offer programs where retired teachers can teach abroad or help improve educational infrastructure in underserved communities.
Educational Foundations	Many educational foundations and non-profits focus on improving education worldwide. Volunteer with these organizations to support their mission and initiatives.
Professional Organizations	Join educational associations or professional organizations that have volunteer opportunities. These organizations often have committees or working groups where you can contribute your expertise.
Mentor New Teachers	Support novice teachers by offering mentorship and guidance. Many schools and districts have mentorship programs that pair experienced educators with those who are just starting their careers.

When considering volunteer opportunities, think about your passions and areas of expertise. Tailor your volunteer work to align with your interests and the causes that matter most to you. Volunteering not only benefits the community but also provides a sense of fulfillment and purpose during retirement.

Final Thoughts

Over the last year, I have had the opportunity to be a part of ASCD's inaugural group of Champions in Education, or Edchamps, which is a program that helps mid to late career teachers define their impact. Part of what has drawn me to this group and has kept me engaged is the consideration we have taken as a group about the way we want to leave education at the end of our careers. Also, it's great to be with an amazing group of educators who each make me want to be better at what I do. When I came into education, I knew I wanted to make an impact and leave a legacy, but I'm not sure the path became clear as to how until several years into my career. My passion for assessment emerged as I saw the injustices that were happening to some of my students and I wanted to do better. It's with that reality that I have continued to move forward, find my people, and continue to courageously restart, getting involved in areas that I didn't even know were available when I started.

 REFLECTION QUESTIONS

- What is your current impact in your career?
- How can you ensure that the impact you make outlives your physical presence?
- How has education changed over the course of your career and how have you stayed nimble within it?
- What do you feel your professional obligation is to leave lasting change?
- Who do you have in your life that can help you navigate what comes next?

Afterword

Courageously Restart

As I'm finishing this book, I'm struck by how much I miss the excitement and challenges of sharing a learning space with students every day or at least on a somewhat regular basis. No matter how long it has been since I last thanked my students for working with me, I still imagine myself as a classroom teacher and it is likely I always will. That doesn't mean I don't love working with teachers; it is just different. As a matter of fact, I'm fortunate to have great relationships with the schools I work with and the teacher teams I've been lucky enough to collaborate with. And in the same way a student could light up my day by telling me how much they enjoyed a class, a teacher in a building telling me they are excited I'm here on a professional learning day also fills me with joy. In fact, on a trip I've taken recently, several teachers shared how much they appreciate our time together; they commend me on how much they feel heard and this is a high compliment as I work hard to ensure that they do.

One of the amazing parts of being an educator is that we have so many options in how we spend our time. It is both routinized in some way and different which keeps everything exciting and busy. The energy is palpable and I appreciate that. There is nothing better than the hum of a functioning school.

As our exploration courageously restarting comes to an end, I am reminded that the journey of transformation in education is not a destination but an ongoing process. The path we've treaded has illuminated the way for educators to

 DOI: 10.4324/9781003450702-13

embrace change, shift their paradigms, empower their students, and engage in reflective practice. Now, in this concluding chapter, we delve deeper into the essence of courage and resilience required for such a transformative endeavor.

The Courage to Innovate

Courageous restarts in education necessitate a willingness to innovate. It involves stepping out of the comfort zone and venturing into uncharted territories. Educators must summon the courage to experiment with new teaching methods, technologies, and pedagogical approaches. They need to accept the possibility of failure, recognizing that every misstep is an opportunity for growth. As we navigate the complexities of the modern educational landscape, it is this spirit of innovation that will drive progress. Since we are all aware of how we have to do this with kids, we have to be bold enough to reinvent ourselves as often as needed to stay relevant in our lives and the circles we place ourselves in. Choosing different pathways should suit the time of life you are in and your current lived experiences. Stay brave in your journey. The most exciting part of change is the opportunity to learn new things and make important contributions to the world.

Resilience Amid Challenges

Challenges are an integral part of any transformative journey. Educators who embark on courageous restarts may face resistance, skepticism, or setbacks along the way. They must cultivate resilience to persevere through these trials. The ability to bounce back from adversity, adapt to changing circumstances, and maintain a steadfast commitment to student-centered learning is what separates the courageous restarters from the status quo. Remember the messages we have always given to students - don't give up. Think about the posters that I'm sure adorned the walls of your classroom, take a page out of your own book and don't give up. Starting over and facing adversity is hard - but not insurmountable. Find your people and lean on them as you move into this new phase of your career.

A Lifelong Learning Ethos

Thought leaders remind us that the process of courageous restarts is deeply rooted in the concept of lifelong learning. Educators must model this ethos for their students, demonstrating that learning is a lifelong pursuit. As they adapt, evolve, and grow in their careers, educators inspire their students to do the same. It is through this commitment to continuous learning that the seeds of transformation in education are sown. Hold fast to your growth mindset and when you believe you can't because it gets hard, remember you can. It's just a matter of perspective most of the time. Wipe away your expectations that can silently work against your forward movement and believe that wherever you end up, it will be exactly where you're supposed to be. And the best part is, if it isn't you can always change your mind and do something else.

The Collective Impact

Courageous restarts are not solitary endeavors but collective movements. Educators, as agents of change, must come together, share their experiences, and amplify their impact. Building a supportive network of like-minded colleagues, collaborating on innovative projects, and advocating for learner-centered approaches are critical components of this collective effort. The transformation of education is a shared responsibility, and it is through collective action that lasting change is achieved. The people I have found in this iteration of my career have helped me see my own growth, inspired me to keep pushing on, and challenged me to do better. It wasn't only the adults and colleagues in my life who have put my impact in perspective, but the students who have reached out over the years to remind me of how much our shared learning impacted their choices and/or created purpose in their lives. Some of these students have even become English teachers. This is the highest compliment and how we ensure that legacies move with us.

The Call to Action

As we conclude our exploration of how we can courageously restart in our careers, I am issuing a call to action. The time is ripe for educators to be catalysts of change in education, to embrace the journey of courageous restarts, and to lead the way for future generations of learners. The challenges are great, but so is the potential for impact.

In the words of countless educators who have embarked on courageous restarts, let us heed the call to innovate, to persist in the face of challenges, to embrace lifelong learning, and to recognize the power of collective action. As we do so, we embark on a transformative journey that will reshape the landscape of education, making it more student-centered, inclusive, and responsive to the needs of the 21st century. The future of education is in our hands, and it is a future worth courageously restarting for. Whether education is where you stay or you branch out into something completely different, know that your voice matters and you got this.

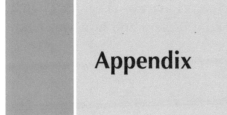

Appendix

Position Proposal Template 1

Position Proposal

Overview:

Job title:

Job focus:

Job description:

Evaluation of the position: (Consider how your new
position will be evaluated)

Qualifications
-
-
-
-

Position Proposal Template 2

Job title:

Location:

Proposed time:

Ongoing consulting support

Salary suggestion:

Overview:

Job specifications and responsibilities:

Remote responsibilities:

On-site responsibilities

Hybrid

Appendix

Proposed Schedule Template

Monday	Tuesday	Wednesday	Thursday	Friday

Proposed Responsibilities, Possible Activities, and Benefits and Outcomes Template

Responsibilities	Activities	Benefits and Outcomes

Resources for Family Advocacy

Educators who want to become effective family advocates can benefit from a range of resources that provide guidance, knowledge, and strategies for working collaboratively with families to support students' educational success. Here are some valuable resources for educators looking to become family advocates:

Professional Development Workshops and Courses:

- Many educational institutions and organizations offer professional development workshops and courses on family engagement and advocacy. Look for opportunities to enhance your skills and knowledge in this area.
  - www.aje-dc.org/training/
  - https://spanadvocacy.org/learning-portal/
  - https://spanadvocacy.org/programs/pti/
  - www.projectappleseed.org/workshop--professional-development-
  - www.copaa.org/page/AdvocateTraining
  - www.pta.org/home/advocacy/advocacy-resources/Advocacy-Training
  - https://fcsn.org/trainings/

Books and Publications:

- *Beyond the Bake Sale: The Essential Guide to Family/School Partnerships* by Anne T. Henderson, Karen L. Mapp, Vivian R. Johnson, and Don Davies.
- *A Teacher's Guide to Communicating with Parents: Practical Strategies for Developing Successful Relationships by* Suzanne Capek Tingley.
- *The Parent–Teacher Partnership: How to Work Together for Student Achievement* by Scott Mandel and Marsha Speck.

Websites and Online Resources: Explore websites and online platforms that offer a wealth of information, resources, and tools for family engagement and advocacy. Organizations like the National PTA, Harvard Family Research Project, and Edutopia provide valuable resources and articles.

- www.pta.org/
- https://archive.globalfrp.org/
- www.edutopia.com
- https://anxietyintheclassroom.org/parents/i-want-to-advocate-for-my-child/school-advocacy-resources-for-parents/

Family Engagement Toolkits: Some organizations and educational agencies create toolkits and guides to help educators build strong partnerships with families. These toolkits often include practical strategies and best practices. For example, the U.S. Department of Education offers a "Dual Capacity-Building Framework for Family–School Partnerships Toolkit."

- https://sedl.org/pubs/framework/#
- https://nafsce.org/page/Toolkits
- www.wested.org/resources/family-engagement-toolkit/

Parent–Teacher Associations (PTAs) and School-Based Resources: PTAs and similar parent–teacher organizations often offer resources, workshops, and support for educators interested in family engagement. Connect with your school's PTA or similar group to access local resources. Check with your local school system for these kinds of resources.

Local Community Resources: Community organizations, non-profits, and local government agencies may offer resources and support for educators seeking to engage with families in their specific communities. Reach out to these organizations to inquire about available resources and partnerships.

Educational Associations and Conferences: Educational associations and conferences often feature sessions and workshops on family engagement and advocacy. Attend these events to learn from experts and network with other educators and advocates. Regardless of whether or not you are in a school, attending conferences helps you stay connected with what is current in education nationally or globally, depending on which conferences you attend.

Parent and Family Workshops: Collaborate with your school or district to organize workshops and sessions specifically designed to educate parents and families about the importance of engagement and advocacy. Encourage parents to attend and share their insights.

Mentorship and Peer Support: Seek guidance and mentorship from experienced educators who have successfully built strong partnerships with families. Learning from their experiences can be invaluable.

Research and Studies: Stay informed about research and studies related to family engagement in education. Research findings can provide insights into effective strategies and practices. Look for peer-reviewed journals and reports from reputable sources.

- https://files.eric.ed.gov/fulltext/ED587534.pdf
- www.k12insight.com/resources/national-report-on-parent-school-trust-and-engagement-aug2022/
- https://files.eric.ed.gov/fulltext/ED362271.pdf

Webinars and Online Courses: Many organizations offer webinars and online courses on family engagement and advocacy. These convenient online resources can provide practical tips and strategies for educators.

- www.trynova.org/training/
- www.family-advocacy.com/events/
- www.brazeltontouchpoints.org/learning-to-advocate-for-children-and-families/
- www.standpointmn.org/webinars
- https://transfamilies.org/familyadvocacy101/

Local Parent Advisory Groups: Some school districts have parent advisory groups that provide insights and feedback on family engagement. Consider joining or collaborating with these groups to better understand parent perspectives.

Facebook is a good starting place for local parent advisory groups.

Remember that effective family advocacy in education requires building trust, fostering open communication, and understanding the unique needs and backgrounds of each family. Continuously seeking out resources and learning opportunities can help educators become more skilled and empathetic advocates for their students and their families.

References and Resources

Alphonso, G. (2023, August 4). *Council post: Empowering learners and protecting privacy: Advancing data security in EdTech.* Forbes. www.forbes.com/sites/forbestechcouncil/2023/08/02/empowering-learners-and-protecting-privacy-advancing-data-security-in-edtech/?sh=49a3b4d13053

Mollenkamp, D. (2023, May 18). *As number of Edtech providers grow, some say student privacy needs a reset.* EdSurge. www.edsurge.com/news/2023-05-18-as-number-of-edtech-providers-grow-some-say-student-privacy-needs-a-reset

OpenAI. (2023). *ChatGPT* (August 3 Version) [Large language model]. https://chat.openai.com

Sackstein, S. (2015). *Blogging for educators: Writing for professional learning.* Corwin, a SAGE Company.

Sackstein, S. (2019). *From teacher to leader: Finding your way as a first-time leader without losing your mind.* Dave Burgess Consulting.

Sackstein, S. (2022). *Hacking assessment: 10 ways to go gradeless in a traditional grades school* (2nd ed., Hack Learning Series). Times 10 Publications.

Sackstein, S. (2023, September). *Making an impact beyond the classroom.* ASCD EL Magazine. www.ascd.org/el/articles/making-an-impact-beyond-the-classroom

U.S. Small Business Administration. (n.d.). *Choose a business structure.* U.S. Small Business Administration. www.sba.gov/business-guide/launch-your-business/choose-business-structure

Other Books on This and Related Topics in Other Fields

Bolles, R. N. (2020). *What color is your parachute? A practical manual for job-hunters and career-changers.* Ten Speed Press.

Christen, C. T. (2016). *The changing career of the correctional officer.* Charles C Thomas Publisher.

Guillebeau, C. (2016). *Born for this: How to find the work you were meant to do*. Crown Business.

Ibarra, H. (2015). *Act like a leader, think like a leader*. Harvard Business Review Press.

Krumboltz, J. D., & Levin, A. S. (2019). *Luck is no accident: Making the most of happenstance in your life and career*. Jossey-Bass.

Miller, K. B., & Ingalls, S. J. (2018). *Designing your life: How to build a well-lived, joyful life*. Knopf.

Tracy, B., & Snell, D. (2017). *Find your passion: 25 questions you must ask yourself*. Berrett-Koehler Publishers.